INSIDE THE TENT
FORTY-FIVE YEARS ON PARLIAMENT HILL

by
Tom Van Dusen

with Susan Code

Published by

GENERAL STORE
PUBLISHING HOUSE

1 Main Street Burnstown, Ontario, Canada K0J 1G0
Telephone (613) 432-7697 or 1-800-465-6072

ISBN 1-896182-86-0
Printed and bound in Canada

Cover design and layout by Derek McEwen

General Store Publishing House
Burnstown, Ontario, Canada

No part of this book may be reproduced, stored in a retrieval system or transmitted in any form or by any means, without the prior written permission of the publisher or, in case of photocopying or other reprographic copying, a licence from CANCOPY (Canadian Copyright Licensing Agency), 6 Adelaide Street East, Suite 900, Toronto, Ontario, M5C 1H6.

Canadian Cataloguing in Publication Data

Van Dusen, Thomas
    Inside the tent: forty-five years on Parliament Hill

ISBN 1-896182-86-0

    1. Van Dusen, Thomas.
    2. Canada – Politics and government – 1935-
    I. Code, Susan, 1960-   II. Title.

FC601.V34A3 1998   971.064'092   C98-900354-X
F1034.3.V25A3 1998

For Shirley, my wife,

and

Tommy, Mark, Tina, Julie, Peter, Michael and Lisa

for their long-standing support and understanding

What fools these mortals be . . .

— Puck, *A Midsummer Night's Dream*

Table of Contents

	A Word to the Wise	viii
1	Laying the Chief to Rest	1
2	Meeting John Kennedy	11
3	Igor Had Problems	15
4	Helping Grattan	19
5	So This is Paris	27
6	The Chief's Tuxedo	33
7	Inside Lester Pearson	37
8	The Chief Lives On	45
9	In the Caribbean	49
10	They Call It the Press Gallery	53
11	The Stanfield Enigma	61
12	The Cameras Move In	67
13	Infallibility and Other Ailments	73
14	One Good Turn Deserves Another	81
15	Working With Allan J.	87
16	Man From the Yukon	95
17	Joe Clark—"Look: No hands!"	103
18	Pierre Trudeau—A Man for All Seasons	111
19	John Turner to the Rescue	119
20	At Home with Brian Mulroney	123
21	Trouble in Paradise	133
22	The Face of Scandal	139
23	With Mulroney in Barbados	149
24	The Parliament Buildings	155
25	Goodbye, Again	161
	About the Authors	165

I'd rather have the sonofabitch inside the tent pissing out, than outside pissing in.

> Attributed to President Lyndon Johnson
> of the United States

A Word to the Wise

This is partly about John Diefenbaker, partly about Brian Mulroney and Allan MacEachen, Mitchell Sharp and Bob Stanfield. Erik Nielsen is in it as are Bob Coates and Sinc Stevens.

Pierre Trudeau appears and disappears enigmatically like a genie from a lamp.

It is partly about the Parliamentary Press Gallery, a curious organization of which I was a member for several years, and about the media that cluster on Parliament Hill like bats upside down in a cave.

Charlie Lynch was part of it and Grattan O'Leary and other titans of the past.

They came and went like shadows on a stage and it is my purpose to bring them back, if only briefly, before the floodlights of memory.

All of the above is simply to establish for the record that I was, indeed, inside the tent.

A number of people have written about parliament, its leaders and its followers, without ever having been inside. Much of the writing has been hearsay, second-hand, third-party and outright speculation. It is my intention that, rather than presenting a portrait of a party, to present a picture of the men and women who make up parties—all parties—from a background of personal knowledge and observation.

Politics is people.

It is made up of men and women, not abstractions in political science textbooks. The men and women in politics are as down to earth as those who drove covered wagons across the Prairies a century ago.

If they weren't, they wouldn't last.

Some don't.

The good ones, the realists, the ones with feeling for the country and their fellow citizens, usually do.

And, like it or not, you can't discuss politics in a democracy without deviating into the media, where I also spent a few years of my life.

That, too, is part of this.

In my four decades working on Parliament Hill, I had plenty of opportunities to study politics and politicians, and to come to terms with the ordinary characteristics of greed, envy, rampant ego, self-indulgence and all those curious erratica that make up human nature.

I worked for three prime ministers and five ministers, including George Drew, John Diefenbaker, Michael Starr, Robert Stanfield, Erik Nielsen, Joe Clark and Brian Mulroney on the Tory side, and Allan MacEachen and Mitchell Sharp for the Liberals.

I did a stint in the Parliamentary Press Gallery for the old *Ottawa Journal*, under its boss, Grattan O'Leary, one of Canada's greatest newspapermen.

I survived these and all the other trials incumbent upon having an artist wife, seven brilliant children, running twice for the Tories in Quebec, and writing and publishing two books.

In 1991, forty-four years after my first appearance on the Hill, I walked out of Prime Minister Brian Mulroney's office for the last time. As I looked around those final days, the miracle was that I was still around.

I had been inside not one tent, but several. Now, I was outside.

CHAPTER 1

Laying the Chief to Rest

ON A CRISP October night in 1991 in the city of Ottawa, six men met for a macabre dinner. All had played a part, more than a decade earlier, in the last rites of John Diefenbaker, his last ride across the country he loved to his last resting place on the Prairies he called home.

Those present were Major General M.G. Cloutier, Sergeant-at-Arms of the House of Commons; Graham Glockling, from the Protocol Division of External Affairs; Robert Coates, the Minister of National Defence in the Mulroney government and a close personal friend of the Chief's; Greg Guthrie, John Diefenbaker's former personal advisor; our host, Brian McGarry, who had been in charge of the state funeral; and myself, former executive assistant to the Chief. Joe Clark, who was prime minister when John Diefenbaker died and who gave the eulogy, could not attend because of the pressure of other duties.

The Chief was gone, but everyone at the table cherished memories of the last days when the entire country bade farewell to the leader whose concern was always for the men and women in the workshops and on the farms of the nation.

He manifested this concern when he campaigned on the streets of the towns and villages: walking into drug stores and barber shops, making himself available to Canadians on the sidewalks and in the shopping centres. There were always a few words while standing on the corner from the man who had known Churchill, Eisenhower, Kennedy and a host of this century's great men.

As we remembered the last epic ride across the Prairies, it emerged that the RCMP reported a bomb scare during the service in

Christ Church Cathedral in Ottawa. Prime Minister Joe Clark made the decision to carry on with the service.

"They can't hurt him now," was his reported comment.

The Chief wanted the Red Ensign to drape his casket. The protocol authorities felt that a state funeral demanded the official Maple Leaf. Diefenbaker had fought against the new flag in the House for twenty-seven days. In the end, the two flags were sewn together and both adorned the Chief's casket.

John Diefenbaker's death came midway through Joe Clark's nine-month term as prime minister. In one month, he would have been eighty-four. The Chief ran in the 1979 election and won, although he suffered several minor strokes. He delivered speeches of which he couldn't remember a word, although he was told they fully lived up to expectations.

In the months prior to his death, the Chief involved himself busily in the arrangements for his own funeral. He seemed fascinated by the details, far more so than by an election campaign.

When Joe Clark became prime minister in May of that year, the Chief went down the hall in the Centre Block and claimed an office that he fancied. Unfortunately, perhaps, it belonged to Jeanne Sauvé, who had been a minister in the defeated Trudeau government. Madame Sauvé did not take kindly to her office being pre-empted by John Diefenbaker. She promptly complained to the Sergeant-at-Arms, who informed her that the Tories, now in power, had taken over the office.

I found the Chief ensconced behind a desk in a room with powder-blue walls and drapes, and a cream-coloured carpet, looking as out of place as a cactus in a rose garden. He was busy writing as he waved me to a chair and called out to his secretary for a copy of the "Funeral File."

"Whose funeral, Mr Diefenbaker?"

"My funeral."

The Chief began with great gusto, describing Abraham Lincoln's posthumous train ride to Springfield, with ceremonies in Baltimore, Philadelphia and New York—a journey of two weeks across the continent. The Chief seemed fascinated. I found it rather unsettling. When he began dwelling with some relish on Mackenzie King's last ride to Toronto, after lying in state in the Hall of Honour, I broke in.

"I'd prefer not to talk about your funeral, Chief. If you don't mind."

"You're very sensitive."

When I left a few minutes later, he was on the phone to External Affairs, lining up the protocol requirements for a state funeral.

He researched his own funeral, just as he did every other important matter. In fact, I don't think I've ever seen anyone enjoying his own funeral quite so much as John Diefenbaker. When it finally took place, he would know more about the procedure than anyone else there. He wouldn't, however, be in a position to share his knowledge.

That was what hurt. I didn't relish the idea of the Chief passing away, like a giant tree of the forest, leaving around him an empty space, littered with the detritus of lesser growth.

A few months later, I got a phone call at my home in Russell, Ontario, about twenty-five miles south of Ottawa, from Archie McQueen, a Hamilton school teacher and friend who was staying with the Chief. It was 7:30 a.m. The date was August 16, 1979. John Diefenbaker was dead.

They had found him sprawled on the floor of his study, surrounded by a litter of papers for a speech he was to deliver that evening at the opening of the Dempster Highway through Roger's Pass in the Rockies. When I got to the house on Lansdowne Road in Ottawa's Rockcliffe Park, they were wheeling out the Chief, covered in a white sheet. It was an inexpressibly melancholy scene. The Chief's small, white dog, McCandy, was running up and down, barking. He knew something was terribly wrong.

My world stopped.

He had dominated the political scene in my adult lifetime as an eagle dominates the space he flies in. He was Everyman blown up larger than life, but with the kind of space and public attention that Everyman seldom gets. The very force that drove him, however, sometimes made him intransigent, demanding and unwilling to listen to reason. He often did things the hard way because in his book, that was the better way.

John Diefenbaker had no patience with theories about "Two Nations," or "Associated States," or any of the mumbo jumbo that proposed to divide the nation along lines of race and language. Such proposals he described as the balkanization of Canada. He believed in One Canada, with freedom and equal rights for every man, woman and child.

While John Diefenbaker lay in state, crowds flowed through the House of Commons, across the Rotunda, down the steps and under the Peace Tower. They were Canadians from every walk—farmers, public servants, media—some whose families had been here for generations and others whose rich accents denoted their more recent arrival. A great man of their time was no more. Lubor Zink, columnist, positioned himself on a walkway above the casket and took a photo. It showed the Chief's features in a marble repose, hands folded, a look of ineffable calm.

Questions were raised about Edna, his first wife, and why he chose to be buried alongside Olive in the grounds of the University of Saskatchewan. Such decisions are so much a part of individual privacy that only those involved can comment. I thought his decision spoke for itself. Shirley and I had met Edna when she first came to Ottawa. She was a friendly, outgoing, bubbly politician's wife, urging reporters to "write about John." Many did.

Eventually she suffered the trauma of a politician's wife: alone in the house in Prince Albert, having to do everything for herself—even putting coal in the furnace—while John waged his brilliant career in Ottawa. There she felt unwanted and out of place and, eventually, she was confined to an institution.

Politicians are generally self-centred; this creates problems in their marriages. Furthermore, it is in the nature of political life to impose never-ending demands. A politician is usually married to the job, which means that the wife or husband of someone engaged in politics must face a serious rival: not another person, but the demands of the voting public.

I know of more than one political wife who ended in an institution and others who, borne down by the stresses and strains of political life, terminated their own lives.

Neither of the women John Diefenbaker married bore him children. I always had a feeling the Chief would have liked a child to carry on his name. He had a tendency almost to adopt some of the people around him. George Hees was a personal defection that hurt him badly, because he had viewed George almost as a son.

When Edna Diefenbaker was briefly in Ottawa following a period of institutionalization for mental strain, Shirley and I were invited to dinner at the downtown apartment where she and her husband lived. I was still a member of the Parliamentary Press Gallery and on friendly terms with John Diefenbaker, who had recently come into the House as a backbencher from Lake Centre, Saskatchewan.

Others who attended the small dinner that night were Bob Taylor of the *Toronto Star*, Arthur Blakely of the *Montreal Gazette*, and Dillon O'Leary, Gratton's son, who was working for a Vancouver paper.

Edna was vivacious and friendly, very concerned about John and his career and insistent that we should all be writing more about John and his outstanding performances in the House. A few years later, she died of leukaemia.

The Chief was in Australia on a parliamentary mission when Edna entered her final illness. He hurried back in time to be present at her deathbed.

Speaking of the ravages of the then little-known disease, he told me many years later, with horror in his voice, that he witnessed the blood actually seeping through her skin.

One Saturday morning at Stornoway, the Chief, happily married to Olive for a decade, talked about Edna for the first and only time. We were in his study working on notes for a speech in the House when, out of the blue, he suddenly spoke of the sorrow and anguish of his life with Edna.

"No one will ever know what I went through with Edna."

He told me that, during an argument with her, he had walked off the elevator at the third floor, where the old Press Gallery was located. Edna had stayed on the elevator, shouting down the corridor after him, "You're not even a man."

In all the years I knew him, I saw the Chief with tears in his eyes on only three occasions: when they lowered the Red Ensign from the Peace Tower; when, six months after Olive's death, he complained of utter loneliness; and on this day, recalling his humiliation from a decade earlier.

* * *

In the last great train campaign during the 1965 election, we covered the same route as the Diefenbaker funeral train did fourteen years later. How different this time, with the Chief lying in state in the baggage car behind, the casket draped in two flags and guarded by members of the House of Commons security staff, men who knew and admired him.

I walked through the train as we crossed the Prairies. Through the windows, I could see farmers on their tractors, hats over their hearts in that age-old gesture of respect for the dead.

I found a group of reporters and political mourners on the train. Southam columnist Charlie Lynch was playing "Red River Valley"—the Chief's favourite—on his ever-present harmonica. These were men who had deep connections to the Chief and who deeply mourned his loss. Men like Don Mazankowski, Joe Clark, Steve Paproski, Alvin Hamilton, and Ray Hnatyshyn.

Ray Hnatyshyn's father, John, was a Saskatoon lawyer known as the Ukrainian Diefenbaker because of his speaking style and the streak of white in his dark hair. In 1967, he had died virtually in the Chief's arms while talking to John and Olive in their suite at the Bessborough Hotel in Saskatoon.

John Hnatyshyn seldom needed a microphone. Mike Starr told a good story about himself and John visiting the Ukraine after John was made a senator. Each wanted to go to his home village and since they were close to each other, they went together on a pilgrimage in search of roots. A large and formidable Intourist woman was assigned to them who insisted that she share a compartment with Mike. In a panic, Mike insisted that he could not leave his friend, Senator Hnatyshyn.

"So, you two are that way, are you?" the Intourist guide leered knowingly.

Mike hastened to assure her that the only thing that bound them together was a mutual regard for Conservative principles.

The sad part of the story is that Senator John Hnatyshyn did not live to see his son, Ray, become Governor General of Canada.

On the funeral train, I sat with a group of trainmen who talked about John Diefenbaker and how they got to know him as he travelled back and forth to Ottawa. Elsewhere, however, dissension began to appear as the Tory mourners got down to their favourite sport of fighting amongst themselves. The atmosphere soon assumed that of a Viking funeral; emotions boiled up as the bereft followers fought the old battles over again, resurrected old scores, measured loyalties, and claimed identification with the dead leader. Some took credit for their unswerving loyalty to the Chief through the years; others, they felt, had not been so demonstrably loyal. By the time the train got to Saskatoon, the only person everyone was speaking to was Senator Al Graham, representing the Liberal Party.

I found men in tears and reminded them the Chief didn't approve of emotional displays; they agreed and dried their eyes. One long-time supporter complained bitterly about being called a "son of a bitch."

"You've been called that before."

"Not on a funeral train."

In the Valhalla to which his warrior soul had hurried, I was convinced that the Chief's only regret, if he had one, was that he was missing his own funeral.

Official pallbearers at John Diefenbaker's Funeral: Dr Samos, Tom Van Dusen, Col Robert Huston, Greg Guthrie

In Prince Albert, the entire town turned out to pay respects to its favourite son. Greg Guthrie leaned forward, peering at the silent crowd lining the street, viewing the cortege with its flag-draped casket.

"This is one of the best crowds the Chief ever had."

Prime Minister Joe Clark delivered a simple eulogy on the grounds of the University of Saskatchewan as the two caskets, John and Olive's (she had died two years earlier and her casket had been moved from Ottawa to be by the Chief's), were lowered into the ground.

"In a very real sense, his life was Canada."

Even at the graveside, controversy made its appearance. Two pipers showed up, one sent by the party in Ottawa, the other by local Tories. I suggested they should both play. I had no authority, of course, to make suggestions, but I felt it was better than having them come to blows.

The Chief's Last Ride. A sorrowful Tom Van Dusen, official pallbearer at John Diefenbaker's funeral, watches as the Chief's casket leaves Parliament Hill for the last time.

A few moments later as the pibrochs faded, a group of Natives appeared and began chanting. A university official told them to desist. I asked what they were chanting.

They answered, "Lament for a Dead Warrior."

Again, with no authority, I intervened.

"The Chief would like that. Carry on."

The university official stalked away, looking miffed.

As the caskets disappeared into the ground, a pair of wild ducks flew out of the slough, circled over the graves and, with a flutter of wings, headed high into the heavens. I looked at the Natives and they looked at me. We had seen an omen.

The Chief and Olive were at rest.

* * *

Returning to Ottawa after the funeral, the tension and sense of loss seemed to lift as we gathered on the prime minister's aircraft. Prime Minister Joe Clark was chatting with Jim Jerome, Speaker of the House in the Trudeau government, and a man liked and admired by the Tories, not only because of his ability as Speaker, but because of his talent as a piano player. When the Tories came to the Speaker's summer residence at Meech Lake, Jim Jerome played and the late Steve Paproski, Member for Edmonton Centre, and Lincoln Alexander, Member for Hamilton West, sang. Steve expressed regret at the thought of losing Jim Jerome's services, should he be replaced as Speaker.

"It would be too bad to lose him," I agreed.

"Where will we find a piano player of his calibre?" Steve asked.

I got one of those brilliant flashes for which, in my own mind, I was becoming noted.

"Why don't we name Jim Speaker? The media would play it as a step towards a permanent Speaker. Joe would get credit and we would keep our piano player."

Steve's face lit up. He grabbed Joe Clark by the arm.

"Why don't we keep Jimmy on as Speaker?"

"Okay by me," Joe nodded agreement. "What about it, Jim?"

"I have only one life to give to my country."

It was settled. Jim Jerome was unanimously voted in as Speaker, to the plaudits of the media. It meant that Clark, with a minority government, did not have to give up one of his badly needed members to sit in the Speaker's chair. It also meant that Steve Paproski and Lincoln Alexander maintained access to a great piano player.

* * *

A curious contretemps took place when the Chief's will was probated. It turned out that he had named Greg Guthrie, Keith Martin (his executive assistant at the time of his death), and me his literary executors. We understood this to mean that we would supervise the publication of his papers, as Jack Pickersgill had done for Mackenzie King. It was not to be.

The Chief, who was constitutionally incapable of doing anything simply (like most lawyers), had made us his literary executors, but had left his papers to the University of Saskatchewan. In the ensuing court case, a judge ruled that power over the collation, selection and publication of the papers went to whoever had been given the papers. The lawyer representing the university went so far as to suggest the Chief had named us merely to register his appreciation of our services, without intending that we should actually assume control.

We didn't fight the issue as strongly as we might have. None of us relished the responsibility of going through the huge mass of documents that John Diefenbaker had left behind. I had actually scanned most of the Chief's papers in a cursory way before his death, when they had been sent to the National Archives. I counted some 1,220 large cardboard containers. We received the judgement with a heartfelt sigh of relief.

In 1968, I wrote in my book, *The Chief*:

> . . . he gave to the arid world of politics unaccustomed zest and colour, standing out in the silted sea of Canadian public life as rugged as the Inchcape Rock. After Diefenbaker, the grey tide crept in . . .

Time has given me no reason to alter that opinion.

CHAPTER 2

Meeting John Kennedy

ON NOVEMBER 22, 1963, Greg Guthrie, the Chief's parliamentary advisor, and I were lunching with John Diefenbaker in the Parliamentary Restaurant when the announcement came that President John F. Kennedy had been shot. Although they had had their personal disagreements, Diefenbaker admired the young president for his courage and idealism.

Horror-stricken, he left his food on his plate, jumped up and went down to his office. Guthrie and I followed at a more leisurely pace. When the House convened at two o'clock, the Chief was ready. Speaking after the prime minister, Lester Pearson, he delivered a heart-felt eulogy, using the phrase coined by Secretary Stanton on the assassination of Abraham Lincoln:

"Now, he belongs to the ages."

Due to the grim circumstances of the day, it was singularly appropriate.

My thoughts were on the young president I had met in the Oval Office in the White House, two-and-a-half years earlier. Our visit followed a speech in which the president called automation the supreme industrial challenge of the decade. Arthur Goldberg, United States Secretary of Labour, had previously come to Ottawa to confer with Labour Minister Michael Starr, for whom I worked as executive assistant, on the Canadian Winter Works Program and our program to fund new technical schools across the country. President Kennedy had expressed an interest in both projects.

Here are the notes I scribbled down on my return to Ottawa on Friday, April 18, 1961:

Returned from Washington last night . . . I met and shook hands with President Kennedy, a dynamic and highly keyed person. He was in the midst of the Laos and Algerian crises. The French Ambassador was in his office. He came out on the terrace and chatted. Had picture taken with Mike and Labour Secretary Goldberg. Two children were being taken into dinner by nurse accompanied by Secret Service man since recent kidnapping scare . . .

Secretary Goldberg took us around on the lawn behind the Oval Office and the president came through the French doors on the verandah.

"Come in, A'thur and bring your guests."

The famous Boston accent was unmistakable. The president's young daughter, Caroline, was playing ball on the lawn with a shirt-sleeved Secret Service agent wearing a shoulder holster. I wondered what kind of a country it was when a little girl needed to be protected by an armed man. Dallas, a little more than two years later, provided an answer.

Afterwards, Arnold Heeney, the Canadian ambassador, took Mike Starr to the Canadian embassy in his limousine for a reception. Secretary Goldberg pulled up in his limousine: "Can I offer you a lift, Tom?" I gratefully accepted.

Eighteen months later, President Kennedy was locked in the Cuban missile crisis. American naval vessels were ordered to intercept and turn back Soviet warships carrying nuclear warheads. Soviet leader Nikita Khrushchev was convinced that Kennedy would back down. When the United States warships appeared on the high seas, racing to intercept the Soviet ships, it was Khrushchev who blinked. The Soviets turned back.

On October 20, 1962—two days before the crisis began—Prime Minister John Diefenbaker received a telegram from President Kennedy condemning in strong terms Canada's proposed intention to support the United Nations in a moratorium on nuclear testing. He concluded by saying:

> Mr Prime Minister, I cannot over-emphasize my concern in this matter and for the reasons I have advanced above and in the interests of a vital Western solidarity on this testing issue, I hope you will reconsider this decision to cast an affirmative vote for a resolution which can only damage seriously the Western position on an essential issue of Western security.

Mr Diefenbaker felt that the difficulty in the nuclear arms issue was national sovereignty. If Canada could have forgotten that we were a free, sovereign nation and accepted the American conditions, we could have jumped on the nuclear bandwagon.

In the end, the Soviets backed down and Kennedy's firmness caused Khrushchev to lose face, costing him prestige with his own generals and naval commanders, from which he never recovered. It also engendered lasting bitterness on his part against John F. Kennedy. Thirteen months almost to the day after the showdown in the Caribbean, Kennedy was dead, brought down by an assassin's bullet in Dallas, Texas. The man who killed Kennedy — dishonourably discharged United States Marine, Lee Harvey Oswald — had returned to the United States after spending eighteen months in the Soviet Union. He brought back with him a Russian wife at a time when it was virtually impossible for Russian citizens to leave the Soviet Union.

In his analysis of the Warren Commission Report, which examined Kennedy's assassination, famous trial lawyer Louis Nizer noted:

> His shots were at the chief symbol of world order and power, the President of the United States. He was not firing at John F. Kennedy. He centred in his gun-sight all mankind, which in his disordered mind, had betrayed and rejected him.

This psychiatric analysis provided a convenient out for the Warren Commission, which wasn't prepared to link Oswald with the Soviets. The fact that Oswald had spent eighteen months in the Soviet Union was treated as inconsequential in the Commission's report. However, less than a year after John Kennedy was shot, Nikita Khrushchev was out of office.

In his memoirs, *The Vantage Point*, former president Lyndon Johnson wrote:

> I was certain that the reason for the abrupt change in Soviet leadership was not Khrushchev's health, as the Soviet News Agency, TASS, claimed. There were deeper reasons for the shift.

And one reason was that after Kennedy's assassination, Nikita Khrushchev had become a liability to the Russian leadership.

Chapter 3

Igor Had Problems

NO ONE could deny that Igor Gouzenko was both courageous and an idealist. A Soviet cipher clerk who defected from the Soviet embassy in Ottawa in September 1945 with lists of potential spies, his revelations touched off one of the major espionage probes of the Cold War. Afterwards, Gouzenko—one of the more enigmatic characters of this post-war period—slipped out of sight, becoming a country gentleman in rural Ontario. Whenever he appeared on television or in court, he wore a hood or brown paper bag with eyeholes punched through to protect his identity.

His wife, Svetlana, a Ukrainian girl, often dropped in to see Mike Starr when he was Minister of Labour. Also of Ukrainian background, Mike did what he could to help get the Gouzenkos settled in his own rural Ontario riding. Igor himself came to John Diefenbaker's office on several occasions and then Dief used to send him down to me.

I first encountered Igor as a cub reporter on the *Ottawa Journal*, covering the trials of those he had named. One of my jobs was to run hot copy back to the office for Greg Guthrie in time for the noon edition. Guthrie had just returned to his old reporting job after five years of knocking around Italy and France as a major in the armoured corps. We hooked up again years later when he came on board as special advisor to John Diefenbaker.

Guthrie would hand me a bunch of copy paper with one or two sentences on each sheet and I would then rush downstairs to a waiting cab to drive to the *Journal*, where the city editor, Dick Jackson, would edit and send up Guthrie's prose to be set in type.

The technology lacked the panache of modern electronic coverage, but, nevertheless, *Journal* readers who stood in line in downtown Ottawa to buy the five o'clock edition received the full story of the afternoon's revelations in condensed, concise and readable journalese. Compared to today's skimpy sound bites overlaid by the comments of a TV reporter, *Journal* readers got good value for their five cents.

In addition to this courier service, my connection with the Gouzenko spy probe was ephemeral, with the exception of a few smash-and-grab raids on the apartments of various individuals in order to obtain photos for the *Journal* front page.

I was instructed by my city editor to get photographs of some of the people named by Igor. This entailed, on at least one occasion, a break-and-enter by myself and the *Journal*'s demon photographer, T.V. Little.

Tommy Little came equipped with a complete set of burglar tools, so it was the work of a few minutes to open a kitchen window in an Ottawa apartment and hoist ourselves over the sill. We combed the apartment looking for photos and then prepared to leave by the front door, like civilized book salesmen. However, Little, with that prescience for which he was noted, first opened the door and applied an eye to the crack.

Then, what to his wondering eye should appear, but the back of a scarlet tunic worn by an RCMP officer. Silently, he shut the door and turned to me, finger on his lips. I needed no warning. Like thieves in the night, we retreated by the same window we had entered. We had our pictures.

Some of the people exposed by Igor Gouzenko had world-wide espionage connections. Their evidence led to the arrest and conviction of two Soviet agents living in Britain, Klaus Fuchs and Alan Nunn May, both of whom had turned over nuclear secrets to the USSR.

When Igor defected, he left the Soviet Embassy, walked over to the *Ottawa Journal* and tried to interest the night city editor, Chester Frowde—"The Man in the Green Eyeshade," as he was dubbed by the press—in a briefcase full of files revealing the names and activities of Canadians spying for the Soviets in key defence areas. I worked night staff under Chester and, early on, came to the conclusion that the one thing Chester feared was a red-hot story.

One of the kindest newsmen in the business, the word for Chester Frowde was caution. He told Igor that the *Journal* didn't handle defections; he should go to the RCMP. Igor did so and found even less interest there.

So, discouraged and afraid, Igor wended his way home to his wife on Somerset Street and presently had visitors—a car full of KGB from the Soviet Embassy who wanted to know what the hell he was up to. Hearing the subsequent row, neighbours summoned the police and Inspector Duncan Macdonnell of the Ottawa Police Force arrived and took charge. First, he kicked out the Russians; then, he placed Igor and Svetlana under police protection. In the morning, they were taken in charge.

Shortly afterwards, the Minister of Justice, Louis St Laurent, came on the scene. St Laurent needed no convincing. He immediately realized the significance of the information conveyed by the Gouzenkos. They were held incognito and the roundup of suspicious persons began. However, St Laurent's biggest problem was Prime Minister Mackenzie King, who didn't want to hurt the feelings of Stalin and our Soviet allies by breaking the spy story.

Canada had just come out of six years of war against Nazi Germany with the USSR as one of our allies. It was hard for Canadians to realize the Soviets had their own agenda and that they were ready to capitalize in any way possible on any weakness the West might show. Even before hostilities broke out in 1939, the Soviets had begun developing a world-wide espionage system, which they refined and expanded under the cover of world war. Gouzenko was among the first to lift the corner of the Iron Curtain to reveal the Soviet machinations taking place behind it.

So, a Royal Commission was established. The people named by Gouzenko were held incommunicado without benefit of legal counsel. A number came to trial.

Igor came to see the Chief in the '60s, when the Tories were in opposition, and he, in turn, sent him to my office. There Igor sprawled on the sofa and told me his financial troubles resulting from his belated discovery of credit cards. Igor thought credit cards were a marvellous example of the finer workings of democracy. And, despite the success of his book, *The Fall of a Titan*, he had run up bills all over the place. Then came time to pay.

Igor was short, with faded blond hair and thick glasses. When he appeared on TV, he usually wore a hood. He lived on a farm in southern Ontario, where the RCMP had provided him with a new identity. A friend of mine in the Security and Intelligence Branch complained that Igor had proved a handful when he was in a "safe house" in the Gatineau Hills during the spy probe. Igor did not like the RCMP cooking. So, they told him to get breakfast himself, which he did and promptly burned the sausages.

The Chief put what pressure he could on the Pearson government and something was done to temper the wind to the shorn lamb of Igor's financial problems. A few years later when the CBC wanted an interview with Mrs Gouzenko, she flatly refused until my son, Mark, approached her. This was after Igor had passed away and a new regime had assumed power in the USSR. I was proud to learn that she agreed because, "your father was the only one who ever did anything for Igor."

I rather liked Igor and I could readily understand his frustrations. Dealing with the Canadian bureaucracy must have at times reminded him of Moscow.

Chapter 4

Helping Grattan

MY ADMIRATION for Grattan O'Leary, editor of the *Ottawa Journal* and Senator, was a factor in my newspaper life from the beginning until his death in 1976 at the age of eighty-seven.

Born in Gaspé, Grattan left school at age twelve to work as a kid reporter on a New Brunswick paper. Two years later he graduated to political reporter on the *Journal*, beginning an association with that paper that lasted the rest of his life. Under his editorship, the *Journal* gained a nation-wide reputation for its editorial writing and Grattan became a force in national politics long before his appointment to the Senate.

Entry to the Parliamentary Press Gallery in those days was based on competent and effective reporting. When I first got there in 1947, the strange hydra-headed monster known as the media had not appeared. There were only print journalists in the Gallery and most of those were giants in the profession, who had come up the hard way through police and court room coverage, fires, accidents, crime, politics—the entire gamut, in short, of news coverage.

O'Leary himself was a case in point.

A feisty little Irishman who visited Ireland twenty-six times, he delighted in setting up court in an Irish pub to lecture the denizens on their own history. Volatile, sparkling and witty, Grattan based his editorial style on the best British prose writers, including Thomas Babington MacAuley, John Morley, Gladstone's biographer, and the Irish essayist, T.P. O'Connor. Under O'Leary's inspired guidance, the *Ottawa Journal* became the most quoted newspaper in Canada.

Grattan entered the profession just after the Boer War when the leading international correspondents of the day included Winston Churchill, Conan Doyle, Richard Harding Davis and Edgar Wallace. Grattan wanted to be better than any of them. He was sent to New York to interview survivors of the *Titanic*, covered the Parliament Buildings Fire of 1916 and eventually became editor of the *Journal*. As a young reporter, he interviewed Sir Wilfrid Laurier lying on a couch in the Victoria Museum in Ottawa surrounded by exhibits in glass cases. This was when the House of Commons took over the museum after the great fire.

O'Leary's appearance in the *Journal* newsroom about seven in the morning, vest open, cigarette dangling, and hair parted in the middle was a signal that the news day had started.

Although a confirmed Conservative who felt that Arthur Meighen could do no wrong, O'Leary played golf with the great Liberal minister, C.D. Howe. (This was in the days when journalists had not yet made a fetish of keeping politicians at a distance.) And, during the Second World War when his son was reported missing, it was Prime Minister Mackenzie King who phoned Grattan personally to give him the sad news, a measure of the high regard in which he was held.

One of my early assignments under Grattan O'Leary was to cover George Drew's campaign in Ontario and Quebec during the general election of 1949. I knew that he admired the Conservative leader and wanted him to defeat the Liberals under Louis St Laurent, who had inherited the leadership from Mackenzie King. Grattan had given the keynote speech at the 1948 Conservative convention that elected Drew over John Diefenbaker. (Grattan said that one of the Toronto organizers had told him the exact number by which Drew would win.) These were more than usually troubled days for the Tories. Drew was the fifth man in ten years to lead the party, but he had a proven track record. He had won Ontario three times.

I reported daily to the *Journal* on the Drew campaign and my write-ups, to say the least, were enthusiastic. Drew was attracting crowds. When I reported that Drew lured 8,000 people to the Quebec City Armouries, Grattan was thrilled. Drew hardly had a word of French, but with that subtlety for which the Tories have been noted, they assigned Drew's charming and gifted wife, Fiorenza, to say a few words in French. Daughter of Edward Johnson, director of the Metropolitan Opera, the tall, soignée Mrs Drew stepped onto the rough platform outfitted in a designer gown and crowned with a chapeau by Mainbocher. There was respectful, even awed silence during Mrs Drew's speech, which she delivered in impeccable Parisian French. Putting her on a political stage in Quebec was the equivalent to having Margaret Thatcher speak for a candidate in Truro, Nova Scotia.

What Grattan failed to realize was that politics in Quebec is a blood sport and people turn out to see candidates the same way they would turn out to see Mohammed Ali or George Foreman—sporting instinct and curiosity. Therefore, no amount of cajoling could persuade them to support the candidates sponsored by an English-language army colonel, who actually looked and talked like an English-language army colonel, rather than those of "Uncle" Louis St Laurent. The fact that 8,000 people turned out to see George Drew didn't mean that they would vote for George Drew. Most didn't.

The Liberals coasted to a landslide victory over the Conservatives in all regions of the country but the new province of Newfoundland.

A consummate speaker, Grattan's only rival was John Diefenbaker. They neither liked nor trusted each other, despite their shared political allegiance. There may have been an ingredient of mutual jealousy in the relationship.

O'Leary was always fascinated by politics and yet, the only time he ran, he was defeated. Diefenbaker admired great writing and desperately tried to put his sometimes circumlocutionary phrases into hard, punchy prose. He rarely succeeded.

When the Tories finally did form the government under John Diefenbaker, Grattan and I were one day sitting in his cluttered office on the sixth floor of the old *Journal* building on Queen Street. He told me that unless the Chief named him to the Senate in the very near future, the prime minister would lose his paper's support. The *Journal* had supported the Tories since the days of R.B. Bennett in the 1930s and its support of Diefenbaker had been, at best, lukewarm. I dutifully repeated this demand and accompanying threat to Alastair Grosart, National Director of the Conservative Party, with the added comment that there was no doubt in my mind that O'Leary meant what he said. Alastair at this time was riding high as the genius behind Diefenbaker's victory in the 1958 election. Alastair had also been on the Drew campaign train a few years earlier, a woebegone picture of disaster. Politics is like that. Down one day, up the next.

Nothing happened. It wasn't until he was well into his second term with a minority government that the Chief finally broke down and made the appointment. Even then, Grattan got up in the Senate to say that he owed Diefenbaker and his government nothing. Everything he had gained, he had won by his own efforts. Probably quite true, but not particularly grateful. It has often occurred to me that one of the few real sins in this world is ingratitude. When the party, with its usual graciousness tried to dump Diefenbaker as leader in 1963, Grattan rushed to his defence. A year later, he sided with the dissidents.

The only disagreement I ever had with Grattan O'Leary was during the year we worked together on his book. It, naturally, involved the Chief.

Long after I had left the *Journal* (in fact, I was working for Allan MacEachen), Grattan got in touch with me and asked to see me in his Senate office. He wanted my help in writing his memoirs. He had a contract with a publishing firm, but was unable to fulfil it. He had learned of a spot on his lung and, at age eighty-six, an operation was not feasible. He got on television and announced his own coming death—expected in the next year or so. This was an unusual step, but perfectly in character. However, such was my respect and admiration for Grattan O'Leary that there was very little I would not have done for him. I was, in fact, rather flattered at being asked to work with one of the foremost journalists of my lifetime.

A prominent Canadian publishing house applied for a grant to the Canada Council to cover writing expenses. It was turned down. It was not the Council's year to support distinguished Canadian editors. However, a Canadian businessman based in London put up the money for the book on the understanding that his name would not be revealed. It never has.

I bought a tape recorder and got eleven-and-a-half hours of Grattan O'Leary on tape—no small achievement—going on about his early days in the Gaspé, his arrival at the *Journal* and the big stories he had covered. I had a transcript made, cleaned up some of the expletives that punctuated Grattan's telling of the episodes, charades and political assassinations he had witnessed over the years. We argued occasionally. In the first place, I got him off his original idea, which was to write about the prime ministers he had known—*Laurier to Trudeau*, or some such title. I told him someone had already done that.

"Anyway," I continued, "nobody cares about all that. Politicians are dull as ditch water. Why don't we do Grattan O'Leary?"

"Who would read it?"

"Everyone, Senator. You're a household word."

He was. He had just conducted a filibuster in the Senate, holding up a bill to increase unemployment insurance payments on the ground that people were being paid not to work.

He came round to the idea and we set to work. However, as we began taping, he announced that John Diefenbaker would rate only an asterisk. For some reason, I found this amusing and couldn't help grinning.

"I know you don't agree, but that's my view," Grattan said tersely.

Over the years, our most persistent disagreements had centred around the Chief and, likewise, with the Chief over Grattan. Quite frankly, I was getting a little tired of trying to sell Grattan on the idea that the Chief was all heart and thought highly of him, and countering the Chief with the notion that Grattan was more to be pitied than censured.

"Senator," I replied, "in my lifetime, I've had the privilege of working with two great men. Diefenbaker is one and you're the other."

"Bullshit."

It was Irish against Irish. I could see by his face that he wasn't totally displeased, so I went home and wrote what I considered a fair, impartial chapter on Diefenbaker. I showed it to Grattan, who harumphed and said he would consult a friend over the weekend. I knew he meant Dalton Camp, then installed as writer-in-residence at Queen's University in Kingston. Camp had an inborn dislike of Diefenbaker, which dated back to his term as National Director of the Tory Party; Dalton felt that the Chief treated him like a minion and, therefore, he had been instrumental in the leader's downfall. However, I also knew that Dalton would be fair and that he appreciated good writing.

I met Grattan in his Senate office.

"My friend says this is fine."

He flashed me his impish Irish grin and I looked down with an equally Irish deadpan. The chapter could go in as written. Dalton Camp was astute enough to know that if Grattan came out with a book on his times and the outstanding figures he had encountered—and omitted John Diefenbaker—nobody would look foolish except O'Leary.

I was having lunch with the Chief a few days later when I told him, "I'm working with Grattan on his book."

"The little bastard," he uncharacteristically replied.

"He's dying of cancer, Chief."

Quick as a flash, came the change of mood.

"Poor little fellow."

A few days later, we went up to the alcove regarded as the Chief's private table in the Parliamentary Restaurant. Grattan was sitting with friends at a table in the very entrance of the alcove. The Chief avoided looking at him and Grattan acted as though the Chief wasn't there. I found the performance between the two grown men like something out of an old *Our Gang* movie. I talked to Grattan and then sat with the Chief, feeling a bit like a herald caught between two hostile soldiers at the Battle of Crècy. This may be a slight exaggeration, but the whole scene was unreal.

I thought, it's a game. How can they take it so seriously? I thought about it for awhile and put it down to ego. Men with larger than life personalities had larger than life egos. Perhaps that was one of the reasons why the Chief distrusted Pearson. He seemed entirely free of ego. The Chief felt all that selfless bonhomie had to be a pose. Diefenbaker had his portrait painted by Cleve Horn, a spectacularly gifted Canadian artist. It hangs in the entrance to the House of Commons and shows the Chief in his robes as an honourary doctor of the University of Punjab—larger than life, almost overpowering in a splash of crimson. The companion piece of Lester Pearson shows him in an innocuous business suit, crouching in an almost fetal position and diminished by the wide expanse of canvas. It seemed to the Chief to perfectly reflect the man.

Now, both O'Leary and Diefenbaker are gone. Two men, giants rather, each with his own particular qualities. One, a great newspaperman, the other an outstanding public figure. Both driven by a quest for perfection in human affairs, and discovering only the human comedy. Both gifted beyond the ordinary, both compulsive in their attachment to destiny. They couldn't be friends, the Gaspé lad and the boy from the Prairies. Although I'm convinced each had a sneaking admiration for the other. Perhaps in some remote Valhalla beyond the stars, they are debating, shaking fingers in each other's faces, settling the fate of humanity. I like to think that may be the case.

Inside the Tent

Chapter 5

So, This is Paris

IN 1950, as a young reporter, I was sent by the *Ottawa Journal* to Paris to cover the first scheduled overseas flight by Trans Canada Airlines (later Air Canada). It was a long, noisy and tedious flight, comparable to crossing the Prairies in a covered wagon.

Years later at a reception in the House of Commons, I spoke with Claude Taylor, former chairman of Air Canada, who remembered the TCA North Star landing in Moncton, where he was airport manager.

"A historic journey," he called it.

I boarded the North Star feeling somewhat like Columbus in reverse, I told Claude. We had a passel of journalistic notables aboard, like Gillis Purcell, the iron-fisted general manager of Canadian Press; Georges Langlois, of *La Presse*; Maurice Nantel, of *Le Canada*; and Dennis Braithwaite, of the *Toronto Star*. We also had D. Leo Dolan of the Canadian Travel Bureau and Walter Turnbull, Deputy Postmaster General.

You had to shout to make yourself heard above the American-built Pratt and Whitney engines that had been put in the aircraft to replace the normal Rolls Royce engines called for in the British design. Tory leader George Drew had tried to make an issue of the North Star's engines in the 1949 election. The problem was that the number of Canadians who had flown in the aircraft could hardly fill a hall, much less carry an election. Consequently, he limped into Opposition with only forty-one members. A friendly guy once you got to know him, George had a tendency to latch on to issues of little interest to anyone but himself.

We put down at Gander and again at Reykjavik, Iceland. I have a matchbook proving that I have, indeed, been to Iceland, if only for an hour.

In Paris, we landed at Orly Airport to discover a city bubbling with spring. All of the romance in the world was concentrated in one heady whiff. It was the 2000th anniversary of the *Ville Lumiere* and General de Gaulle's brother was mayor. Hollywood couldn't have improved on the cast.

At the Hôtel George V (where I stayed, courtesy of TCA), I went up in the open grillwork elevator expecting to hear strains of Ernst Lubitsch on every side. Music there was none, but the operator was completely in character: he wore a long, blue coat with epaulettes and a look of quiet heroism. He had undoubtedly fought in the Liberation.

I decided to try out my Gatineau French and found we conversed with little effort. This was surprising, because all kinds of people who didn't speak French had warned me about using Canadian French in Paris. They would look down their noses and, if not satisfied, would say brusquely, "Zut, alors!" I had no intention of being made the butt of anybody's "Zut, alors!" particularly a Paris Frenchman.

My conversation with this impressive elevator operator soothed my concerns. Obviously, he was a graduate of the best schools. I congratulated him and he responded,

"Vous venez du Canada, Monsieur?"

"Oui, Monsieur."

"De quel endroit?"

"La ville d'Ottawa."

"J'ai vécu vingt-six ans sur la rue Stewart."

My confidence evaporated as though at a waving of a wand. Here was this bum telling me he lived on Stewart Street in Sandy Hill, an upscale Ottawa neighbourhood, for twenty-six years! No wonder we spoke the same French. I resolved to be very careful to whom I spoke.

I soon had other problems.

The room TCA had reserved for me was rather palatial. There are no other kinds in the George V. And, in those days, with the war just over, there were no journalistic reservations about accepting handouts or freebies from corporations, even government corporations. That's what corporations were for. Surely, they didn't expect me to fly over to Paris at my own expense to cover TCA's inaugural flight? Let's be reasonable. The *Journal* had given me $500 to cover expenses so, since TCA was paying for everything, there shouldn't be any expenses. How little I knew.

In the marble-tiled bathroom, I found two toilets. This was a puzzler. One for English, one for French? Male and female, perhaps? I tried the first one and got squirted; the other one appeared to be normal. I found out later that the first bowl was a French institution known as *le bidet*. Its purpose remains obscure to this day.

That night, I came down with a raging fever. My doctor had warned me that there might be a reaction from smallpox shots, which were mandatory on a journey to Europe. With visions of an old story about smallpox sufferers being walled up in a Paris hotel room during the Great Exposition a century earlier, so as not to put a damper on the festivities, I shuddered to think what might happen. Still, I had no intention of dying like a dog in the Hôtel George V, miles from home.

I called down to the desk to say that I wasn't feeling well. Then, I blacked out. I woke to find a woman with very blond hair in a white, starched uniform bending over me. It didn't take long to figure she must be a nurse. A man in a red jacket was standing beside her shining a flashlight in my face. I wondered what a Paris doctor was doing in a red jacket. He later turned out to be the night elevator operator.

When I opened my eyes, he switched off the flashlight and turned on a bedside lamp. The nurse told me I had a fever. Since I was covered with a light film of sweat, I could not disagree. Somewhat to my surprise, she said she would rub my chest with Vicks. I found this an innocuous remedy for someone suffering from smallpox. However, I decided to submit. The man in the red jacket went away (possibly because the elevator bell was ringing), and the nurse and I were alone.

She opened my shirt and began industriously rubbing me with Vicks. I felt she was taking the entire situation far too lightly. I decided to level with her.

I told her I had had a *piqure* (vaccination) before leaving Ottawa. Then I mentioned the dreaded word, *variole* (smallpox). She didn't seem to care. She didn't seem to care about anything. She just went on, rubbing away with the Vicks. She told me that during the war, if it hadn't been for Vicks, half the population of Paris would have perished.

She gave me an aspirin and said I would be better in the morning. Then she left, taking the jar of Vicks with her.

She was right. The next morning I felt better, much better. In fact, I was well enough to board a train at the Gare de Lyons for a trip to Britanny.

We sat in the club car and drank wine with an attractive girl in a ski costume, returning from a ski holiday in Switzerland. Her brother was with the French Army at Dien Bien Phu, Indochina. When the Americans went in a few months later, it became Vietnam. I had a copy of that day's *Figaro* in my bag, announcing the capture of Dien Bien Phu by the Communists. I decided not to show it to her.

She left the train and drove off in a big, old Rolls Royce with glittering headlights and a uniformed chauffeur who assisted with her skis. As the train moved off, the car rolled up a long avenue of Lombardy poplars towards a château right out of *The Three Musketeers*.

We went to Rennes and St Malo. In Rennes, we visited a large stone church, the floor paving worn down by the feet of many centuries. In St Malo, we went to Jacques Cartier's house, by now preserved as a heritage site. And we visited the great rock of Mont St Michel rising out of the shining sea with a monastery on top looking as though it had grown out of the rock itself.

At Mont St Michel, we stopped at Mère Poularde's where I discovered the secret in making an omelette lies in the wrist action. We received a demonstration when the sous-chef walked right into the great fireplace and whipped the eggs with a wrist action reminiscent of Navratilova on the court.

We careened round the roads of Britanny on a bus singing *Alouette* with the Chamber of Commerce of St Malo for whom, apparently, the song was a favourite.

I also discovered a lot of separatists in Britanny, people of ancient Celtic descent who still had the language so much so that, during the war, they could converse in Gaelic with the Welsh.

Back in Paris, I met my first prostitute, a large girl in a red coat marching down the Champs Elysees at midnight. Dennis Braithwaite and I said, "Bon soir, mademoiselle." She stopped and said something in French.

"What did she say?" Dennis asked.

"She wants us to go to her bureau."

"What for? Is she selling licence plates?"

"Not quite."

"Where is her bureau?"

I posed the question and the girl answered.

"Across town. You take the metro."

I decided that it was too far and too late. I had visions of a couple of apaches pouncing on us once we left the security of the bright lights. Dennis shrugged and went back to the hotel.

I got into a small Citroen taxi and told the driver to take me somewhere.

He took me to St Germain des Prés.

There I dismissed the taxi with a lordly gesture and walked the narrow, twisting streets of the Left Bank, crowded in spite of the late hour with waves of students chanting and rocking little French cars, sometimes tipping them over, regardless of the screams of the drivers.

I found the pointlessness of this exercise rather boring and walked on until I encountered a blast of sound and heat from an open doorway. Looking down, I saw a long staircase and crowds of people dancing: an underground bistro. I went down to where a group of black girls in wide, colourful skirts and kerchiefs were dancing on a stage. To a passing waiter, I asked, "Qui sont ces femmes-la?"

He stared at me for a moment, then his face cleared.

"Ce sont des femmes de la Martinique, monsieur."

It was my first encounter with the Caribbean, a place on the earth's surface that has greatly enriched my life.

To a frantic burst of calypso, I wove through the crowd to a table where a blond girl in a white turtleneck sat with two sailors. She was a reporter from the Argentine newspaper, *La Prensa*, which had just been closed by the dictator Juan Peron. One of the sailors was a nephew of Eduardo Cavalcanti, the Brazilian filmmaker. I bought champagne all round (courtesy of the *Ottawa Journal*), which arrived in a bucket packed with ice in the best Hollywood tradition. We chatted and watched the show.

People were dancing, some black, some white. Nobody seemed to care. The reporter had just returned from skiing in Switzerland. It seemed that every girl I met in Paris had been skiing in Switzerland.

I left about an hour or so later. I needed sleep. The sky had begun to pale across the Seine where the tower of Notre Dame pointed like a finger in the dawn. The cobblestones glistened with rain. I wig-wagged a cab and went back to the George V, just in time for bed.

Le Figaro reported that Lauren Bacall and Humphrey Bogart were in Paris on their honeymoon. They had a picture to prove it. Georges Langlois met me in the lobby and said that Humphrey and Lauren were in the bar. I was too tired to care.

"Tell them I'm out here."

They didn't come out. So, I went to bed.

Searching for Downed Flyers. Tom Van Dusen (far right), as a young reporter on the Ottawa Journal, joins a search for flyers missing in the Quebec bush.

CHAPTER 6

The Chief's Tuxedo

AFTER HE LEFT the leadership, Olive Diefenbaker persuaded the Chief to buy a new tuxedo, to replace the one he had worn since the post-war Bretton Woods Conference in San Francisco some twenty years earlier. He offered me the old one. For historical reasons, I accepted.

I remember the Chief wearing the tuxedo at a Press Club Ball at the Château Laurier, sometime in the fifties, when he was just John Diefenbaker, a back-bench member from Saskatchewan. It was after the death of his first wife, Edna, and before he married Olive. Charlotte Whitton, Ottawa's feisty mayor, accompanied him as his date. Greg Guthrie was president of the club that year and he and his wife, Norma, shared a table with John and Charlotte.

I have a vivid memory of the occasion, because I won a shirt for a door prize and it was presented to me by Louis "Satchmo" Armstrong, the greatest jazz trumpeter of them all.

The local press, of course, made sly comments about Dief and Charlotte, comments without foundation, since within a few months he married Olive Palmer. However, the Chief maintained a high regard for Charlotte and several years later, after he became prime minister, he intimated that he wanted to name her Ambassador to Ireland. Unfortunately, before the appointment could take place, Charlotte made the front pages by socking an Ottawa controller on the jaw at a council meeting. This ended her diplomatic career before it got off the ground. Charlotte always maintained that the incident didn't damage her image in the eyes of the Irish, and she was probably right.

I wasn't particularly keen on having the Chief's tuxedo; when word got around, I would probably have to go to a lot of functions I wouldn't normally attend.

I want to make it clear that my idea of an exciting evening is to go to bed with a good book, preferably something written before the turn of the last century. I have a soft spot for G.A. Henty, Sir Arthur Conan Doyle and Sir Samuel Baker, whose *Seven Years in Ceylon* remains a forgotten classic. H. Mortimer Batten's *Habits and Characters of British Wild Animals* is hard to beat as a sleep-inducer, while *On Horseback through Asia Minor*, by Frederick G. Burnaby, soldier and pioneer balloonist, is a rip-snorter.

I accepted the tuxedo, however, and took it to a tailor to have it altered, since the Chief was a couple of inches taller than I. When the tailor saw the Chief's name stencilled on the inside pocket, he blanched.

"May I ask where you got Mr Diefenbaker's tuxedo?"

"He gave it to me."

"My God, I thought you stole it."

When I got the tuxedo back, it fit perfectly. It is double-breasted with long, shiny lapels—like the ones favoured by Jimmy Cagney and Humphrey Bogart in gangster movies of the thirties.

It looked good.

It made me feel like the Chief.

I decided to wear the tuxedo to a Press Gallery dinner and walked up Parliament Hill, a symphony of quiet elegance. Another man, also in a tuxedo, fell in beside me.

"You working here tonight?"

I quickly disassociated myself from this interloper, making a big thing of tying my shoelace, so we wouldn't be seen entering the dining room together while he made his way to the kitchen.

However, I continued to wear it to a few places with something of the feeling of being draped in the Mantle of Caesar or the Sacred Shroud of Turin. Then, strange things happened with the Chief's tuxedo.

After the Chief passed on, I took it to be cleaned and pressed, and when I went to collect it, an embarrassed cleaning attendant told me that it had been handed out by mistake to a maître d' at a local hotel. He promised to have it back shortly. This wasn't good enough. The thought of the Chief's tuxedo ushering people into restaurant seats was too much. I fully expected the Chief to come back from the other world and demand his tuxedo from the delinquent waiter.

I dropped into the hotel in question, just to check on the tuxedo, and there it was, lighting up the dining room with its 1930s glow. I got it back a few days later—cleaned and pressed at no charge, none the worse for wear. I think, perhaps, even the Chief was not unhappy at the proletarian service it had performed.

That, however, wasn't the end of the Chief's tuxedo.

A few months later, when the National Press Club decided to honour a distinguished Canadian, Lincoln Alexander, Lieutenant Governor of Ontario, they asked me to be master-of-ceremonies. I suppose they found out I had the Chief's tuxedo.

In fact, Lincoln was an old friend, whom the Chief had personally persuaded to run federally when they met at a campaign meeting Lincoln chaired in Hamilton during the 1965 campaign. My admiration for him is unbounded.

It turned out to be a great evening. Club members, media people and parliamentarians turned out to honour Lincoln and his lovely wife, Yvonne. I performed throughout as master-of-ceremonies, feeling strangely reassured by the fact that I was wearing the Chief's tuxedo.

When it was over, Lincoln thanked me and said:

"You know, you kind of reminded me of John Diefenbaker up there."

I didn't tell him why.

John and Olive Diefenbaker arrive for a visit at the Van Dusen home in Aylmer, Quebec.

CHAPTER 7

Inside Lester Pearson

LESTER PEARSON, known for obvious reasons as "Mike," was a highly regarded public servant who rose to Deputy Minister (Undersecretary of State) for External Affairs under Prime Minister Louis St Laurent.

Pearson was undersecretary when St Laurent turned down the request by Anthony Eden, Prime Minister of Great Britain, for Canadian assistance in the Suez Crisis of 1956. Abdul Gamal Nasser, president of Egypt, had decided to take over the Suez Canal, which had been built by the British nearly a century before under Prime Minister Benjamin Disraeli. St Laurent made the entirely gratuitous and uncalled-for statement to the effect that the time had passed when the "strong men of Europe" could call on the colonies to come to their rescue. The statement was generally recognized for what it was—rodomontade of a peculiarly windy kind. The author was presumed to be the undersecretary, Lester Pearson. Anyway, he did an about-face and earned a Nobel Peace Prize for his efforts in establishing a United Nations Peace Force to intervene in Egypt.

Mr Pearson entered the House of Commons in 1958 as the new leader of the Liberal Party and immediately demanded that the Diefenbaker government, which had achieved a minority status in the 1957 election, step down and let the Liberals take over. Diefenbaker demolished the reckless new leader with scorn, invective and contempt, as only he could, and went on to gain the greatest majority to date in a general election the following year.

I campaigned in the 1958 election with the Honourable Michael Starr, Minister of Labour. As Mike's executive assistant, I accompanied him from coast to coast, searching out and visiting Ukrainian communities on the Prairies, in the Rockies and on the coast.

In the 1962 election, Diefenbaker saw his majority melt away, largely due to cabinet dissension. This, compounded with the controversy over the Bomarc missiles—expensive, short-range nuclear warheads that the Americans wanted to base in Canada—meant that he lost it all to Pearson in an election the following year. In 1963, Lester Pearson became Prime Minister of Canada with a minority government and he named Paul Martin Sr Minister of External Affairs.

I developed a unique insight into Pearson through my own relationship with Paul Martin Sr. I was working for the Leader of the Opposition at the time.

Having suffered polio as a boy in Pembroke, Ontario, Paul was in the habit of walking round the House at noon to strengthen his muscles. Often, he invited me to accompany him. On these walks, Paul talked freely and frankly of his problems and feelings, knowing anything he said would go no further. As a matter of fact, I never repeated or passed on anything he told me.

Paul was often hurt at the way in which the press gave Mike Pearson credit for every forward or positive step in the foreign affairs field, and blamed Paul for the disasters. He felt he was very much in the shadow of the prime minister, who had won the Nobel Peace Prize. As prime minister, Pearson couldn't refrain from acting as his own external affairs minister. However, Paul spoke privately to me of one occasion during the Vietnam War when this backfired.

Pearson had just delivered his famous "Bombing Pause" appeal in a speech in New York. Paul said that the speech was disastrously timed. It came out at the very moment President Lyndon Johnson had rejected the proposal during a discussion with his cabinet. Johnson was furious at Pearson's intervention and virtually summoned the prime minister to his Texas ranch. After flying Pearson and Martin around in the helicopter for an hour to impress them with the magnificent extent of his spread, Johnson read the riot act to Mike. According to Paul Martin, Johnson reminded Pearson that American boys were dying in Vietnam and, as far as he knew, no Canadians were and he would thank Pearson to keep that fact in mind before plunging in with both feet. Paul had never seen or heard of a Canadian prime minister taking such a dressing down from a foreign leader. Pearson took it all, like a recalcitrant school boy, saying very little in his own defence and retiring with what aplomb he could muster. To cap the indignity, Johnson introduced him at a press conference as Mr Holyoke. Keith Holyoke was the Prime Minister of New Zealand.

That was Paul's story, and I believed him. I, of course, did not mention it to anyone.

* * *

Lester Pearson's secretary, Mary MacDonald, was a woman of many fine attributes, including a lively personality and a very well-furnished mind. She invited me once, out of the goodness of her heart, to a reception upon Pearson's return from a holiday with the Rockefellers in the Caribbean. The situation in the House was rather tense at the time. In Pearson's absence, a tax measure imposed by his government had been defeated. Since it was only a surtax, and not a major measure, Pearson resisted demands for an election.

Opposition Leader Robert Stanfield, the enigmatic Nova Scotian who usually showed all the animation of a totem pole, accepted the advice of his aides, Lowell Murray and Joe Clark, and agreed to meet with Pearson to discuss the situation. John Diefenbaker, now merely the Honourable Member from Prince Albert, disagreed. He felt that the Grits should resign or be forced out. Gordon Churchill, Tory House Leader, agreed with the Chief and felt so strongly about the matter that he left the party over Stanfield's waffling.

Pearson arrived and went straight to the reception, where he shook hands with the party faithful and various aides. He looked very pale as he approached and shook me heartily by the hand. He announced that he had been reading a book on the plane called *Fanny Hill*, apparently the reminiscences of a Victorian prostitute. Later, I told the Chief I had been to the reception. When I told him Pearson was reading *Fanny Hill*, he was properly scandalized: "I gollies, has the man no morals?"

Politics was the arena in which John Diefenbaker went out, armoured and panoplied with the justice of the Lord, to do battle with the forces of destruction.

For Lester Pearson, the Chief had the professional politician's horror of the gifted amateur. Pearson, to Diefenbaker, would always be the incarnation of a bumbling bureaucrat who had somehow stumbled into politics almost in spite of himself, and proceeded to make a mess of it. Pearson's own attitude of polite disclaimer seemed to reinforce Diefenbaker's view.

In the 1965 election, when Guthrie and I accompanied the Chief across the country from St John's to Victoria, Prime Minister Pearson started off by saying his government wanted a majority. This was a rather puerile reason for plunging the country into a national campaign and the Chief treated it with the scorn he felt it deserved. However, he made allowances for Pearson on the ground that he was being coached by Walter Gordon, whose grasp of election strategy was on a par with Colonel Tom Thumb's.

Sometime in the early sixties, the Chief received from US Senator Hubert Humphrey a copy of the transcript of Elizabeth Bentley's testimony before the Un-American Activities Committee of Congress. A courier for the communists, Bentley testified that she obtained information from the Canadian Embassy in Washington where Lester Pearson had been counsellor during the war. Since the Russians were our allies, this was not as nefarious in 1945 as it might have seemed twenty years later.

The Chief kept the Bentley transcript in a locked drawer in his desk with just the corner sticking out. At an appropriate time, he would slip the crucial sheet out of the drawer, identifying and summarizing it.

"You know who our ambassador in Washington was? Lester Pearson."

Most people took the revelation rather calmly.

When Mr Pearson, after asking RCMP Commissioner George B. McLellan for a review of security files, dug up the Munsinger Case, involving two of Diefenbaker's ministers, George Hees and Pierre Sevigny, with a German woman of dubious antecedents, Pearson went along to Diefenbaker's office and said he was going to raise the matter in the House.

He had been given this report quite improperly as the files of a former government are not made available to its successor.

Pearson said that Diefenbaker committed a security breach by not firing Sevigny and the Liberals set up a Commission of Inquiry under Mr Justice Spence to investigate the circumstances.

Pearson felt he had a reason for being miffed. His government had been pilloried by Erik Nielsen and Tommy Douglas in the Rivard case (a Quebec heroin smuggler with ties leading to a minister's office), and the George Victor Spencer case. Spencer was a public servant who supplemented his income by selling lists of names taken from tombstones to the Soviets for use in establishing identities for KGB agents. There were also other matters, such as Quebec ministers buying furniture without being billed.

Pearson felt his government had been tarred and wanted some of his own back.

Diefenbaker listened. Then his hand went down to the desk drawer and out came the Bentley statement. If Pearson went ahead with Munsinger, which the Chief maintained had been properly dealt with at the time, then the Bentley allegations would be tabled.

Pearson called his bluff.

The Gerda Munsinger sex and security scandal burst like a thunder-clap on the startled House in March 1966, when the Liberal Minister of Justice, Lucien Cardin, quite deliberately let slip the name "Monsignor" in a heated exchange with Opposition Leader Diefenbaker. Those who heard Cardin, as I did, understood it as "Munsinger." The fact the reference came out in the House of Commons Hansard as "Monsignor" was undoubtedly due to the Hansard reporter's unfamiliarity with the name. But John Diefenbaker had no doubt about Cardin's reference to Gerda Munsinger, a German woman who had married an American baseball player, left him and migrated to Canada where she plied a lucrative trade as a prostitute in Montreal.

A few years earlier, E. Davie Fulton, Diefenbaker's Minister of Justice, was given an RCMP report which revealed that one of Mrs Munsinger's intimate contacts was the Associate Minister of Defence, Pierre Sevigny. The fact that she was German and was known to have contacts with the Russians before coming to Canada could constitute a security risk, but not one the RCMP was particularly worried about. Diefenbaker called Sevigny in and told him to stay away from the woman. Sevigny was furious and his anger later led to his defection from the Diefenbaker cabinet.

Pearson set up a commission to investigate the sexual involvement of the Diefenbaker government with Mrs Munsinger and the Chief let Bentley drop. The twenty-year-old document was, after all, pretty thin gruel. However, he refused to attend the hearings of the Spence Commission and sent Guthrie and me instead. I became very bored with sitting day after day through the monotonous recitals of the haphazard comings and goings of Mrs Munsinger and her friends. Guthrie seemed to enjoy it. The high point came when Pierre Sevigny said he had fallen asleep on Mrs Munsinger's chesterfield. His stock dropped to zero in Quebec.

The Spence Commission was widely regarded as a political court designed to destroy a troublesome opposition. The *Globe and Mail* called the commission's terms of reference "vague, vengeful and prosecutory." In my book, *The Chief*, I dealt in detail with the Spence Commission, its proceedings and its findings.

My own relation with Gerda Munsinger was brief and abruptly terminated. I was invited, along with a friend, to have a drink at Sevigny's apartment in the Beacon Arms Hotel in Ottawa. At the time, I was executive assistant to the Minister of Labour in the Diefenbaker government, Michael Starr. When we got to Sevigny's apartment, he introduced us to two attractive blonds, Gerda and Jackie. However, instead of following Sevigny and his girlfriends to the bar, I followed my reporter's instinct—which has never let me down—turned and left the party. I went down the hall to the elevator, followed by my vigorously protesting friend.

My answer was simple and to the point.

The two girls had Montreal prostitute stamped all over them. Working for a minister, there was no way I was spending an evening in such compromising company. I left the Beacon Arms and headed back to my office in the Confederation Building and my car.

Four years later, the blond called Jackie turned up as a witness before the Spence Commission. She was Jackie Delorme, a Montreal prostitute and a friend of Gerda Munsinger's.

During the hearing, Sevigny introduced the name of John C. Doyle. An enigmatic figure with a pink face and carefully sculpted white hair who lived on the top floor of the Juliana Apartments in

Ottawa behind a shield of armed bodyguards, Doyle described himself as an international financier. He claimed to have ties with Joey Smallwood, the Premier of Newfoundland, and Jack Pickersgill, a former Pearson minister. Sevigny claimed he had met Mrs Munsinger through Doyle. One of the stories that circulated around Parliament Hill was that it was Doyle who tipped off the Grits to investigate George Hees and Pierre Sevigny's relations with Mrs Munsinger. Both of these ministers resigned suddenly and mysteriously from the Diefenbaker government before the 1963 election.

Sevigny told me this story: One night, he got a call from a pal of his who was well-placed in the Montreal rackets. In his friend's night club during the small hours, Sevigny was introduced to a Detroit hit-man who had a contract to knock off Pierre Sevigny. Sevigny's gangster friend warned the hit-man that if he carried out his mission, it would be regarded as an unfriendly act by the Montreal crime bosses. The hit man apologized profusely and headed back to Detroit.

The incident impressed Pierre Sevigny with the value of discretion when dealing with those curious circles that frequent Montreal after dark. Sevigny himself told this story and allowed it to be taped. The only point, really, is to indicate that politics in the sixties was played for keeps.

Sevigny phoned me when the Munsinger inquiry began.
"What should I do?"
"I just had a hell of an idea, Pierre."
"Oh?"
"Try telling the truth. You'll knock 'em dead."
"I'll be the dead one. If I told the truth, I'd end up in Montreal Harbour in a slab of cement."

Sevigny testified and acquitted himself reasonably well. I always had the feeling, though, that he was holding back.

A lot of things went on that I am quite sure the Chief knew nothing about. And, if he heard whispers, he dismissed them as the product of minds inflamed by too many movies.

By the time the Munsinger bombshell hit Parliament, the lady had returned to Germany and, apparently, vanished from the face of the earth. Bob Reguly of the *Toronto Star* found her living quietly in Munich. I asked him how he had accomplished this feat, which had surpassed the capacities of the police of several countries.

"I looked her up in the phone book," he said, "then went around and knocked on her door."

The Spence Inquiry stands as a politically motivated investigation of a former government by its political opponents. No charges were laid. No laws broken. No allegations proved.

Chapter 8

The Chief Lives On

IN 1986, they did something to remember the Chief.

They erected a statue, cast in bronze, larger than life, back of the West Block, where Queen Victoria, on her granite plinth, could look down with approval. The Chief stands, one foot advanced, about to stride away. Just as he was in life.

At the unveiling, Prime Minister Brian Mulroney's voice crackled over the crowd, spelling out the public achievements, homely virtues and innate grandeur of a simple yet complex Canadian. I thought of the days when Brian Mulroney, as a young law student, used to pop into the Chief's office to have a few words with the great man on the political issues of the day, something Brian couldn't seem to get enough of.

After the crowds departed, I went and stood before the Chief's statue. It was surrounded by schoolchildren in bright sunshine who listened while their teacher explained the man's greatness. I, however, thought of the times when I had seen him degraded, cast down. Like in his office in the House on that September morning in 1967 when we left for Maple Leaf Gardens in Toronto where he faced humiliation and defeat.

"They won't vote for a man of seventy-two. What will I do? No one will want to see me."

I grappled for a moment for just the right answer.

"You're still John Diefenbaker. They'll want to see you more than ever."

As it turned out, he was right about one thing. They didn't vote for him. They voted for Robert Stanfield who sat in the stands eating a banana. This was one of Dalton Camp's gimmicks to show the crowd that he was really alive.

Back at the Royal York, the Chief, now a man without a party, gulped down a plate of clam chowder. A few minutes later, he rushed to the bathroom and threw it up.

Politics, they say, is a thankless taskmaster.

They squeezed him out of the leadership like toothpaste out of a tube. Just as they had done to R.B. Bennett, who sat by the phone in the Château Laurier waiting for the call that never came, while the convention picked Robert L. Manion.

The Grits showed a little more delicacy when they sent Lester Pearson down to Quebec to tell Uncle Louis he was through and a leadership convention would be called to replace him. The Tories liked to do their blood-letting in public with all the finesse of a Druid sacrifice.

When I came back from Maple Leaf Gardens with John Diefenbaker, he was no longer leader. He prepared to move out of the Leader's office to a smaller office across the hall, occupied, as it happened, by myself. Having his predecessor crouched like Cerberus, almost on his doorstep, must have irked the unflappable Robert Stanfield no end. Perhaps that's why Dief did it.

Without any doubt, the Chief has been the most impressive figure in Canadian politics in my lifetime. I heard Mackenzie King's last speech, interviewed Louis St Laurent and C.D. Howe, chatted with Maurice Duplessis and Daniel Johnson, and covered Leslie Frost and Bill Davis. Greg Guthrie and I worked for the Chief after he went back into Opposition in 1963. I had run in a Quebec riding in both the 1962 and 1963 elections under his banner and covered him, of course, as a reporter, almost from his first arrival in Ottawa. He was in the mould of great North American leaders, like Abraham Lincoln and Andrew Jackson, although of necessity on a more restricted stage.

There was only one John Diefenbaker. He came from plain, ordinary people of the country and never tried to hide his origins. He spoke glowingly of the sod hut on the Saskatchewan prairie in which his family lived for a while after moving by train from Neustadt, Ontario.

One day, with Ted Rogers of cablevision fame, Diefenbaker and I drove up to Neustadt to see the village and the home the Diefenbakers had left sixty years earlier. It was a big, comfortable looking brick house, shaded by trees on the edge of the village. There were people at home and the Chief, with instinctive delicacy, refrained from going in. We sat outside in the sun taking in the bucolic scene, like a painting by a nineteenth century artist. The Chief let out a sigh and we drove away.

Relieved of the albatross of a political party, particularly one not noted for flexibility or resiliency, John Diefenbaker rose to the heights of leadership. Without the party, Diefenbaker became, in his own lifetime, a sort of folk hero—larger than life. He made the Conservative Party a people's party. The evidence was there in human terms for everyone to see.

Diefenbaker brought both official languages into the House of Commons. However, had he lived to see simultaneous translation—which he installed—become a vehicle for the transmission of separatist arguments aimed at breaking up Canada, he would have writhed in anguish.

It was Diefenbaker who named the first French-speaking Governor General—Georges Vanier—since the Marquis de Vaudreil, the first native—John Gladstone—to the Upper Chamber, the first cabinet minister of Ukrainian background—Mike Starr—and the first woman minister—Ellen Fairclough.

It was Diefenbaker who fought for the principle of a colour-blind Commonwealth where skin colour would not determine a person's place in the social structure and all Canadians, regardless of race, colour, creed or sex, would share the same citizenship.

He had taken a moribund party, lifted it off the ground and hurled it, kicking and screaming over the goal line for its first national election victory in twenty-two years. However, the sight of John Diefenbaker clambering across a beaver dam on a small Pontiac, Quebec, lake, fly rod in hand, was one of the ways in which the measure of the man came through. Once while sitting in a boat on Lake Nipissing with his line in the water, the Chief turned to me.

"I love fishing because no one can phone you here."

It was, perhaps, a novel approach to the ancient piscatorial art. However, while not a fisherman myself as I find fish inescapably dull, I could sympathize with his view.

But, by 1967, the party managers, the image-makers and the big money boys thought they could do better. Perhaps they might have, but their efforts were for naught. Pierre Elliott Trudeau was standing in the wings.

John and Olive Diefenbaker with Lisa and Michael Van Dusen; Diefenbaker staff in background.

Chapter 9

In the Caribbean

IN 1974, the CBC asked me to go down to Barbados and help out on a documentary they were shooting on the Chief. They thought that I would relax him. I had written a book about him and I understood his complex personality. My impression of the request was that they wanted a kind of court jester who would amuse the Chief while they asked tricky questions.

The CBC wanted him away from the House of Commons to where they could work at their leisure. They installed the Chief and Mrs Diefenbaker in a planter's house on the beach that belonged to Mrs Packard, of electric razor fame. She also happened to be the mother of Hollywood actress Lee Remick, whose portraits and busts littered the great drawing room open to the winds from the sea. Olive Diefenbaker spent a lot of time on the patio knitting while the CBC interviewed the Chief in the drawing room.

My wife Shirley came down, paying her own way, and the CBC, in its accustomed, open-handed fashion, installed us in a villa at the Coral Reef beach hotel. We shared it with John Munro, writer-director, and Munro Scott, writer. My position was midway between houseboy and companion. Cameron Graham, a very talented CBC producer, put the show together.

I knew I had an uncle somewhere in Barbados. Uncle Larry had left Ottawa in 1911 to seek his fortune in the United States. He ended up in Hollywood as an interior decorator to the stars, including such marquee blazers as Mary Martin, Anita Louise, Claudette Colbert and Ann Rutherford. We found Uncle Larry, now in his eighties and still working, by the simple expedient of looking him up in the Barbados telephone directory. He came to dinner and presented us with a silver butter dish, a present to my grandmother on her wedding day, December 7, 1870. The dish had travelled from Ottawa to California, then to Barbados. Now, it was headed back to Ottawa, after sixty-three years.

Through Uncle Larry, we were invited to dinner at the Brandts', Americans from Texas, who hosted President Ronald Reagan a few years later. The evening was not uneventful. It was marked by several minor gaffes on my part, which staggered my wife, but were overlooked by everyone else. Like most planter homes, the Brandts' was built around an inner courtyard guarded by an iron gate. Struck by the many outdoor lights, I asked our host what his monthly electric bill was, paying no attention to my wife's kicks under the table. He revealed that it was around $500. Next, I inquired how many furniture factories he owned. He seemed quite happy to admit that the figure ranged in the neighbourhood of fifty-three, several of them in Canada. We dined at a forty-foot-long table, which I presumed was a product of one of those factories. Brandt found that a buzzer attached to the table where he sat wasn't working. After pressing several times to summon their houseboy, Emerson, without any result, Brandt rushed into another room and came back with a screwdriver with which he repaired the faulty fixture. In a few moments, he had it working and Emerson appeared like the genie of the lamp to take orders.

Brandt was from Fort Worth, Texas, where he purchased a condominium tower in the downtown area, in order to live in the penthouse. Subsequently, he purchased a neighbouring tower, so people who could peer across at his penthouse would be people selected or at least approved by himself. This impressed me strongly with the power of American know-how.

Fascinated by these manifestations of high life, I was forced to desist from asking questions because I was in agony from repeated kickings under the table. During the meal, a large dog—a Rhodesian Ridgeback trained to hunt lions—seized writer-director John Munro's wrist, compelling him to eat his meal left-handed. The rest of us, including the Chief, kept our wrists on the table.

One of the reasons why the CBC chose the Packard house, known as Queen's Fort, for Mr and Mrs Diefenbaker was because it was built of coral blocks, which resembled the limestone blocks in the House of Commons, and would provide a fitting background for the Chief. The walls of the House of Commons, however, did not provide small green lizards who made a habit of waiting until the shooting started and then dashing into the frame, as though inspired with a compulsion to immortalize themselves on film.

When this happened, everything would stop and people would chase the lizard back up the wall, out of camera range. The Chief would settle back and John Munro would begin the interview. However, just as things got going, the lizard would appear as though on cue, clinging to the wall behind the Chief's left ear. Pandemonium raged once more, until the intrusive lizard was sent scuttling back to his lair.

Shooting took place in the morning and, after lunch, the Chief would go for a walk along the beach, which appeared to be populated by people mostly from Saskatchewan. Someone would spot the gangling figure with a white streak in his hair and do a double-take. Then they would come forward, first singly or in pairs, then in a kind of mass movement. Everyone wanted to shake his hand. He would invariably ask for names and then give the person in question a kind of capsule history of that person's family. Many reeled back, open-mouthed at this display of total recall.

"Your name is?"

In a hesitant answer would come the name. A large woman in a bathing suit standing awkwardly as a school girl before the legend in bathrobe and towel on a far distant beach in the Caribbean.

"Ah. Your mother taught school in Spiritwood in 1921."

"Yes! Yes!"

Along would come another.

"I knew your uncle. A fine man. He supported me through the years."

It was a bit like a laying-on of hands.

When the crowd faded back a bit, the Chief would doff his bathrobe and step in the water. As he walked out in the surf, swaying slightly, the crowd would sway with him—a sort of sympathetic vibration—like a giant tuning fork made up of many tines.

When the Chief got in up to his waist, he would sway back and forth, like a tree in a high wind, the crowd swaying with him. All of a sudden, he would disappear, ducking into the water for a quick dip. In seconds, he was up, swaying back and forth to the action of the waves. It was at just such a moment that John Turner, coming along the beach, thought the Chief was drowning so dashed in and rescued him from being swept out to Venezuela by the waves. The Liberal Party never forgave Turner for that Good Samaritan act.

Once he had made it back to the beach, the Chief would towel off, go back to the house, dress and accompany us into Bridgetown where he rode up and down the escalator at the Cave Shepherd department store while Shirley and I shopped.

On a holiday, the Chief liked to enjoy himself.

John and Olive Diefenbaker celebrating the Chief's birthday at the Van Dusen home in Aylmer, Quebec, after the 1967 Conservative convention.

CHAPTER *10*

They Call It the Press Gallery

WHEN I FIRST entered the Parliamentary Press Gallery in 1947, I had the good fortune to rub shoulders with many of the great newspapermen of the day. In addition to Grattan O'Leary and Charlie Lynch, there was Frank Swanson of Southam's; Norm Campbell, then of the *Windsor Star*; roly-poly Bob Taylor of the *Toronto Star*; and the redoubtable Evelyn Tufts of the *St John's Telegraph-Journal*. The legendary Bruce Hutchison usually showed up for the Opening of Parliament, an occasion worthy of the trip from his desk at the *Victoria Colonist*, along with Grant Dexter of the *Winnipeg Free Press*, Blair Fraser of *Maclean's*, and Frank Flaherty of the *Chicago Daily News*. Percy Philip, one of the last Americans to leave Paris before the Nazis rolled in, represented the *New York Times* while Gene Griffin held the standard for the *Chicago Tribune*. And there were many, many more.

They had an intimidating affect on me until I discovered they were much like the reporters I worked with on the *Ottawa Journal*, except they had a wider variety of personal experiences. However, they nearly all went out of their way to be helpful to a new boy.

I sat near Ross Munro, who, along with Charlie Lynch and Peter Stursberg, was back from the war. All three were working on manuscripts of their wartime experiences.

When Grattan O'Leary worked in the Gallery in the twenties, there were only twenty members. When I got there, that number had risen to sixty, all print journalists. It was another few years before radio and television crashed the magic circle. As I recall, when I left the Gallery in the early fifties, Tom Earl had been admitted for CBC

Radio. Then came Norman de Poe for television and a horde of hungry, pushy, demanding radio and television reporters whose forte consists of surrounding a subject in a scrum and pushing a microphone into his or her face in order to obtain a "sound bite" for the news. There is no question that when a prime minister, president or minister is involved in a complex and abstruse issue, and someone shoves a mike in front of him or her demanding a forty-second summary, the art of reporting suffers. Public understanding also suffers.

I shouldn't complain, though, since my brother, Jack, and three of my kids have been shining lights in network television. I never got past cable. However, as more and more reporters take it on themselves to interpret in their own words the thoughts, opinions and convictions of elected representatives who are limited to one or two sentences of generally meaningless gibberish, the public tends to downgrade the elected politicians. It instead places its confidence in the people through whose words the thoughts and opinions of the politicians are selectively presented. In the most recent US election, the media took centre stage, treating the two presidential candidates somewhat like backward pupils.

This is not a lament for the good old days and yet, there were giants in the old Gallery beyond those I've already mentioned: Charlie Bishop of the *Ottawa Citizen*, who after his elevation to the Senate was followed by Alex Hume, a bridge partner of the St Laurents; Harvey Hickey of the *Toronto Telegram*, who looked like a cashiered British Army colonel; good, grey, Warren Baldwin of the *Globe and Mail*; Georges Langlois of *La Press*; Maurice Nantel of *Le Canada*; Charlie D'Aoust of *Le Droit*; V.C. Mears and Jim Osler of the *Gazette*; and many others too numerous to mention.

Reporters came to the Gallery after a long and stern apprenticeship in news reporting. There was no thought of stepping out of journalism school and into the most exclusive group of reporters in the country, simply on the strength of being able to hold a microphone and talk in front of a camera. They had to be able to write competently, effectively and clearly in one of the two official languages. They also had to have a proven record of covering the usual round of police stories, fires, accidents, interviews, town meetings, school boards and similar routine activities until, one day, when they had won their spurs and shown an interest in the affairs of the nation, they were sent to cover parliament and become members of the august Press Gallery. In short, you didn't get to cover Parliament Hill until you were a well-rounded reporter, with everything burned, ground and squeezed out of you but a maniacal urge to do news. When this happened to me, I was twenty-five and just married.

I had the satisfaction, a generation later, of finding three of my seven children on the Gallery list: Peter, Lisa and Julie. Tom and Mark were reporters and Tina was getting ready to join the broadcasting industry. Michael went straight and became a lawyer. A good thing. You never know when you might need one.

The approach back then was different. There was no arms-length reporting. You got to know the people you wrote about. I spent considerable time in the office of the back-bencher from Lake Centre, Saskatchewan—John Diefenbaker—just listening. I did the same with Louis St Laurent, Paul Martin, and others. Just like I did with the cops when I was covering the police beat. When I wrote about someone, I knew the man and his beliefs. I drove to meetings with the then leader of the Conservative Party, George Drew, who favoured a roadster with a rumble seat. I also drove to meetings with David Lewis, later leader of the New Democrats, and took down his words as he addressed a crowd of farmers in an agricultural hall, somewhere in the Pontiac, across from Ottawa. This doesn't happen anymore. News is now obtained by osmosis, like covering a bad play that has gone on too long and there is nothing more to say.

When Grattan O'Leary sent me up to the Hill, he gave me some words of advice. *Accept nothing from the government without checking. Never accept a government press release at face value. Dig up your own stories.* I did what I could to follow his advice.

As a novice reporter I was once threatened with expulsion from the Press Gallery for reporting a straight news story, one of the few reporters to be singled out this way. Years later, when serving on the Aylmer, Quebec, town council, a petition was circulated demanding that I resign. Sometimes, I've had the feeling that I might possibly be rubbing people the wrong way.

The occasion was a press conference held by the United States Embassy. Louis Johnson, the United States Secretary of Defense, had called us together so that he could explain a program of arms standardization embarked on jointly by Canada and the United States.

What I knew about arms standardization you could put in your reticule yet here I was, surrounded by veteran reporters, many of whom had been overseas and who had arms standardization at their fingertips.

I found another story that interested me more.

The TASS man in the Gallery was Arkadi Ogorodnikov, a Don Valley Cossack who had served with the Soviet armies. Although a representative of the Russian news agency, he was a very decent fellow and a friend of mine. From time to time, we used to go to a local bar and have a beer. Often, when a government communiqué came out, in the usual indecipherable form, I would explain the gobbledygook to Arkadi.

He became an issue at the American press conference when Louis Johnson stopped in mid-sentence and announced that there was a TASS man in the room and, unless he left, he would cancel the conference. Since there was nothing to stop the TASS man from reading the entire proceedings in the morning papers, Johnson's demand may have been politically inspired. However, looking somewhat sheepish, Arkadi got up and walked out.

The next morning, the *Ottawa Journal* came out with a banner headline: TASS MAN BANNED FROM U.S. PRESS CONFERENCE.

Every other reporter there wrote about arms standardization. So, when the *Journal* hit the streets, they began getting calls from their editors asking where the hell they'd been when the TASS man was kicked out. Curiously enough, the *Globe and Mail* took umbrage at my having the nerve to actually report the news and one of their reporters was so angry that he began to take up a petition to have me kicked out of the Gallery for not properly covering the arms standardization aspect as announced.

Charlie Lynch and a few others came to my defence and laughed this charge out of a closed session of the Gallery executive. I was never certain what sin I was supposed to have committed, other than maybe scooping the ass off the *Globe* and every other news agency, but I was grateful to Charlie. Forty years later, at a testimonial dinner in the National Press Club, I went over to where he was sitting with the newly elected Prime Minister of Canada, Jean Chrétien.

"D'you remember when they tried to get me suspended from the Gallery?"

"Of course I do. I defended you."

"I know you did. I want you to know I've never forgotten."

Jean Chrétien must have wondered what the exchange was all about. It was simple. Two old reporters scratching each other's backs.

Charlie Lynch, a New Brunswick boy, rose to be one of the most authoritative and knowledgeable columnists in Canada. He was honest, fair, with a great sense of humour. A few months after the dinner, Charlie was gathered to his fathers.

Shortly after the US Embassy episode, I attended a function at the Soviet Embassy to view Russian films. (I was working at the National Film Board at the time.) Once the screenings had finished, we adjourned to the ballroom for toasts and, after what seemed only a little while, I found I was the only non-Russian in the room. Everyone was hoisting glasses of pure vodka and shouting out "skol!" I joined in, determined not to be left behind. I then found myself face to face with Borodin, a man generally recognized as the KGB man at the embassy who bore a remarkable resemblance to actor George Raft with slicked back hair, beady eyes and rat face. He began to give me hell about stories I had written for the *Ottawa Journal* while a member of the Gallery. He said they were anti-Soviet. I hoped he was right. They were certainly anti-Communist.

I told Borodin to go to hell. I said Canada was a free country and I could write any damn thing I wanted. Brave words, considering I was trapped in foreign surroundings. Strangely, however, I had the feeling most of the Russians in the room were on my side. I knew they both hated and feared Borodin for his lordly KGB manners.

Borodin turned really nasty. His voice rose and he began shouting. A burly form shoved between me and Borodin—Arkadi. He rapped out a few words, the gist of which I gathered was, "This guy is with me. Leave him alone."

Ruchenko, the naval attaché, took a stand beside Arkadi. Borodin backed off, sputtering. Arkadi turned to me. "Tom, you go home." There was, in fact, no place I would rather go.

Arkadi summoned two large gentlemen from the basement. They assisted me into a limo and we sped away, out the gates of the Soviet Embassy, down Charlotte Street to Laurier, and down Laurier to Bronson Avenue, where Shirley and I lived in an upstairs apartment.

Looking out the window at two a.m., Shirley witnessed my arrival. When she saw me disembarking from the limousine assisted by two large men in caps and military greatcoats down to their ankles, she was certain I was in custody.

No journalism school, no political science course could give the kind of education in the dynamics of politics that the Press Gallery did. I sat in the House, for example, to hear Winston Churchill deliver his famous phrase, "Some chicken, some neck!" I attended his press conference in the Gallery when he summarily put in their places those ambitious Canadian reporters anxious to make a quick name for themselves by tripping the great man up. Sir Winston showed that he didn't trip up.

I attended Sir Archibald Wavell's press conference, while he held the position of Commander of the Free World in the Far East. Seamed and toughened by exposure to the sun that never set, he told how we were winning the war there.

As a member of the Gallery, I sat in the House to watch and listen to the "gentil, parfit knight" of the new Camelot—President John F. Kennedy—while he called on us to ask what we could do to make the world better.

There were also domestic moments, such as when the Minister of Finance, the charming and affable Douglas Abbott, "filled the keg" in the Gallery lounge and went over the intricacies of his budget for reporters who were busily taking notes and drinking his beer.

One night, Dillon O'Leary, Grattan's son, took me up to the office of the Minister of Fisheries, Jimmy Sinclair, whose daughter grew up to marry Pierre Trudeau. Jimmy had recently returned from the Soviet Union where, in the process of inspecting aid shipments, he fell down a hatch and fractured his leg. Showing that he was completely recovered, he put his feet up on the desk and we had a few drinks. Later, after we left, Dillon said,

"That's okay, then."

"What's okay?"

"The story Jimmy doesn't want you to write."

"Oh, yeah. Fine. Quite okay."

What the story was, I had no idea, nor have I discovered to this day. Although, I can't help wondering.

* * *

The Annual Press Gallery Dinner was the social high-point of the season. It was here in the historic sixth floor dining room of the Parliamentary Restaurant overlooking the Ottawa River that the nation's best and brightest got together.

People who had dealings with the media eagerly sought invitations. Industrialists, diplomats and politicians fell over themselves to get a place on the guest list. For on this one night, everyone from waiters to lobbyists enjoyed a temporary truce from the wheeling and dealing that normally went on at the Parliamentary watering-hole.

It was at a Gallery Dinner that Prime Minister Mackenzie King announced his intention to retire (off the record, of course), and then stood in amazement while the Parliamentary Restaurant emptied of newsmen as they raced to find telephones.

It was also at a Gallery Dinner that the cast sang a song about "Harkness's Disease" that so annoyed John Diefenbaker he swore he would never return. Diefenbaker thought they were referring to Parkinson's Disease when they were, in fact, alluding to his problems with Defence Minister Douglas Harkness.

The entertainment following the dinner is distinguished by rude and boisterous songs in which the media get their own back at the politicians. The atmosphere degenerates to the level of a boys' school, along the lines of Dotheboy's Hall in *Nicholas Nickleby*. Quips, insults and, occasionally, missiles fill the air. And woe betide the luckless speaker, usually a politician, who fails to take accurate measure of the mood of the gathering and attempts to derive political advantage.

The preferred method is to make oneself the butt of one's own humour. This can either be done unconsciously, as in the case of Robert Stanfield, or deliberately, as in the case of Ed Schryer when he served as governor general. Jeanne Sauvé, while Her Majesty's vice-regal representative, did an imitation of the Queen, little girl voice and all, which some found inappropriate.

When Erik Nielsen acted as Leader of the Official Opposition in 1983, I prepared what I considered mildly humorous notes for his speech. In keeping with tradition, he was the object of his own punch lines. He wanted a partisan speech with the humour directed at the government and the media. I explained the code of the Gallery Dinners demanded that the speaker must direct his humour at himself. He was having none of this. He wanted to score off the enemy, which included the government and most of the media.

Erik Nielsen wasn't there for laughs. He was there for blood. When the crowd caught on that Erik was taking liberties with the Untouchables of the Press Gallery as well as the Unmentionables of the House of Commons, he almost disappeared under a barrage of buns. In spite of this, he soldiered on to the end and sat down, not even bothering to dodge another volley. If Louis XVI had been executed by a hailstorm of buns rather than the guillotine, the effect would have been similar. Fortunately, buns don't kill. Governor General Ed Schryer, who followed, fared little better. The crowd's blood was up and anyone who appeared did so at his own risk. The governor general escaped with fewer contusions, but only because the throng ran out of buns.

CHAPTER 11

The Stanfield Enigma

ROBERT STANFIELD came in to replace the Chief in 1967, after the leadership convention in Maple Leaf Gardens. I went home to meditate.

After a week or ten days, Mike Starr, who had been named House Leader, called and asked, "What the hell are you doing?"

I said I was building a tree fort for the kids and a fish pond for myself. He said he needed help and I should get my posterior into the office. I said I would work for the members, but I wanted no contact with Stanfield. He didn't impress me.

Truth to tell, my experiences with R.L. Stanfield verged on the uncanny. In 1965, he came aboard the campaign train in Truro, Nova Scotia. I poured him a drink. He never said, "when," so I dripped a couple more drops of Scotch into the full glass, much to the consternation of the Chief. At the leadership convention in Maple Leaf Gardens, when Stanfield was photographed eating a banana, I regarded the performance as almost simian. Following the convention, the new leader appeared like a wraith in my office beside the Chief's and sat staring. Finally, after clearing his throat several times, he allowed that he needed the office. I took it to mean that I should get out, which I did.

At Mike Starr's insistence, I came in and was given an office near the elevator on the third floor of the Centre Block. It was as near as I ever got to the Senate. Whenever the elevator went up or down, my desk wobbled.

The Chief moved into my former office across from the leader, at the head of the stairs on the third floor. He deserved the best.

Joe Clark, Lowell Murray and I worked on Stanfield's maiden speech for the House. Joe eventually became prime minister, Lowell a senator, and I'm retired and living in Russell, Ontario.

I can't help feeling I'm the lucky one.

Stanfield was pleased with Lowell and Joe's lines, but made a point of saying that my material would do for the hustings, but not for the House of Commons. Coming from someone who had never spent a day in the House, this made a big impression on me.

Stanfield blew what should have been an occasion. He put the House to sleep with a dry-as-dust lecture on the economy as filtered through the wisdom of the Harvard School of Economics. In the rowdy and combative House of Commons, this was like throwing him to the wolves. He never recovered. He could have grabbed the House by the ears and shaken it. Instead, he put it to sleep. He said he didn't want to get into political issues. So, that raised the question: what the hell was he doing in politics?

As a businessman and former premier of Nova Scotia, Stanfield was a decent and honourable man. However, he had never learned to struggle.

The House of Commons was not Harvard, nor was his audience comparable to a crowd of docile Nova Scotians awed by the Stanfield name and wealth.

Parliament has never been particularly kind to provincial premiers.

George Drew of Ontario could never capture its heart. Possibly, because as Tory leader, George specialized in four-hour speeches—two hours before supper and two hours after.

Saskatchewan's Tommy Douglas, in the middle of an impassioned maiden speech, was interrupted by a shout, "Get up off your knees!"

The House can be tough, mean and hard on neophytes. Those who succeeded—Louis St Laurent, John Diefenbaker, Douglas Abbott, M.J. Coldwell, Jimmy Sinclair, Pierre Trudeau—took the trouble to learn through experience what the House was all about.

Although Stanfield seemed to have no sense of humour, he was a natural dead pan comic. When I wrote his speech for the Annual Press Gallery Dinner, Stanfield got two laughs for every line. One when he delivered the line; another when he looked up to see what everyone was laughing about.

His major tactical error, which cost him the prime minister's job, was letting the Pearson government off the hook following the defeat in the House of a three per cent income tax surcharge. According to the rules of parliament, defeat of a budgetary measure means defeat of the government. Diefenbaker and Gordon Churchill, Tory House Leader, advised Stanfield to force the Grits into an election, as they had done to the Diefenbaker government in 1963. Stanfield's advisors thought otherwise, so Stanfield decided to wait for Prime Minister Pearson to return from a Caribbean holiday.

Pearson rushed back from the Caribbean, where he was staying as a guest of the Rockefellers, and held a confidence vote in the House, which the Liberals easily won.

Stanfield's action was on a par with a hockey forward picking up the puck in front of his opponent's net and handing it over with a gentlemanly bow. You don't win games that way, either in hockey or in that other great sport, politics. It's a rough, tough business—the people's business—and not to be trifled with. One of the problems with amateurs is they insist on making up their own rules as they go along. That is not to say there is no room for gracious gestures. When Pierre Trudeau cut through red tape to fly Olive Diefenbaker back from the Caribbean where she had taken ill, that was a gracious gesture.

Working for Mike Starr, I prepared speeches for members. I had a system. I filed a number of speech excerpts under headings like constitution, unemployment, foreign policy, agriculture, industry, economy, and so on. When a member asked for a speech, I drew out relevant and appropriate portions and put them together like a jigsaw puzzle. Sometimes, when necessary, I prepared an introduction and a closing. Using this method, I could throw a speech together in minutes. One week, I did speeches for seventeen members of the Tory opposition. My only fear was the dreaded possibility that some night (the House sat at night in those days), two members would give the same speech. Finally, this did happen. Nobody noticed, for the simple reason that the paragraphs were in different order. I concluded that when members spoke, nobody listened.

Politics is a human business; not something to be learned in a text book written by an academic for other academics. Often, leadership is more than a question of policy or political permutations; very often, it is a question of character. People vote for a candidate because they trust him or her.

I now had the impression, rightly or wrongly, that anyone who had remained loyal—come hell or high water—to John Diefenbaker was regarded as untrustworthy by some of the people around Stanfield. I had done what I had to do and had no apologies to make.

In politics, my personal loyalty has usually been for a person, rather than a party.

I first voted Conservative because I lived in a riding where George Drew was a candidate. Also, Grattan O'Leary—editor of the *Ottawa Journal* where I first worked as a reporter—was unabashedly Conservative.

I worked for Allan MacEachen because he had been a friend for many years whom I liked and trusted.

Erik Nielsen was also a friend and a man I admired.

Like me, Brian Mulroney was a Quebec Irishman, and I knew him as a student when he came to visit the Chief.

John Diefenbaker had my personal loyalty because he was someone you could admire and respect. I wasn't happy with the way certain people in the party had worked tooth and nail—even to staging public demonstrations—to force the Chief out. As a silent beneficiary of that process, I had great reservations about Robert Stanfield.

However, nothing so became my brief and inglorious tenure with Stanfield as the ending of it.

One night, I got a call from a professor. He told me that, starting in a couple of days, I would be part of his research group commissioned by the Leader's office. I answered briefly and simply that I had no intention of being part of any group. I sat down and wrote out my resignation, walked down the hall and put it on Stanfield's desk. Next morning, he called. I went down and he said he wanted me to stay on. I was very blunt. I said Diefenbaker had left him with ninety-seven MPs, all of whom regularly visited their constituencies and reported back. Instead of listening to his members, he had surrounded himself with academics and PR types whose political knowledge could be inscribed on a postage stamp. I told him that it wouldn't work and that he would never be prime minister. In a magniloquent finale, I said that I had my reputation to think about.

Stanfield replied in these words:
"The calibre of my advisors is the best answer to your charges."
I couldn't help myself. I burst out laughing.
Then I said, "You have my letter. Please accept it."

On that note, I left the office where I had spent five years working with John Diefenbaker. My heartfelt feeling was one of relief.

On the eve of the 1974 election, Stanfield's advisors introduced a plan calling for price controls. Obviously, they hadn't considered the possibility that price controls might entail wage controls. At the last minute, Stanfield backed off. But it was too late. Trudeau made mincemeat of Stanfield's hazy generalities. The Liberals got the majority they had never succeeded in obtaining while John Diefenbaker was leader.

Meanwhile, I went home to Aylmer, Quebec, and continued working on the tree house for Julie and her friends. I bought a large rabbit in the Aylmer hardware store for one dollar. We called him Harold. Then I bought seven bantam chickens in the same store.

Harold, the rabbit, had charm and personality. He proved it by jumping up on Olive Diefenbaker's lap when she and the Chief came to visit. Eventually, Harold returned to the woods.

Chapter 12

The Cameras Move In

BRINGING CAMERAS into the House of Commons was one of my major preoccupations during the 1970s. First, because I believed taxpayers had a right to be informed about parliamentary issues and judgements by the most effective technology available, and second, because I felt television coverage was the next best thing to being actually in the House.

I had prepared a cabinet document on broadcasting parliament, based partly on a report prepared by John Matheson, formerly a Member of Parliament, at that time a judge. My paper dealt with the technical aspects of organizing coverage, so that all sides of the House and all MPs, no matter where they sat, would have equal exposure, and the proceedings would remain under the Speaker's control. The camera would not be allowed to usurp the functions of the Speaker.

This required eight cameras positioned in the Chamber as inconspicuously as possible, as well as a control room suspended over the Chamber, along the lines of the coverage provided for NHL hockey. A rather ingenious marriage of high tech and traditional Canadian sport.

When Mitchell Sharp replaced Allan MacEachen as President of the Privy Council, he told me to drop everything else and concentrate on bringing television into the House. Sharp believed that television coverage, a kind of "electronic Hansard," would provide a better public understanding of the proceedings and ensure greater accuracy in informing the public. Cameras were allowed into the United Nations. Other legislatures were permitting coverage of special ceremonies. The Speech from the Throne had been broadcast on television for several years. So, the time had come when Canadians from coast to coast to coast should be able to view and hear the debates of their elected representatives on matters of national importance, and not be satisfied with a hasty summary on the late news.

When Minister of Finance, Mitchell Sharp, had been scooped on the contents of his own budget by the media, they emerged from the famous "locked room" and got on air before the minister had finished revealing the budget to the House. Sharp wanted no more of that. Putting cameras in the Chamber meant that ministers making important announcements would be delivering them "live." He felt that bringing parliament into the homes of Canadians would make the House a living institution, rather than a remote and dimly understood relic of the past.

We ran into our first roadblock at the CBC. We were told from the highest level that the CBC had no mandate to put cameras in the House of Commons on a full time basis. However, Mitchell Sharp got around that. He convinced the CBC to lend us the technicians and install the system, if parliament paid the costs. We, however, made it plain we didn't want a system on the cheap. We wanted the best and most up-to-date system money could buy. It had to provide exposure to every member in the House—backbenchers as well as ministers, opposition as well as government—and it had to provide total coverage, in full colour. We eventually got that, at a cost of some $5 million. With the co-operation of the cable industry, we were able to create a parliamentary channel, which was available in forty major centres across Canada, in both languages, reaching a daily audience of 750,000 Canadians.

Of course, there were objections, complaints about cost and showing the House "warts and all." A former Speaker told me, "You will destroy parliament."

One argument that bothered me was the suggestion that the presence of cameras could lead to parliamentary "grandstanding." I told myself there was already grandstanding in the House for the benefit of the media. There could hardly be more, even with cameras. So that argument—and all others—fell before Mitchell Sharp's determination to see the job done.

Speaker Jim Jerome grabbed hold of the idea and ran with it. He set up a special committee of members of all parties and named me advisor to the committee. He enlisted the aid of experts from the CBC, the CTV and the cable industry. Mitchell Sharp brought in Robert Anderson, a film consultant, and Doug Wilkinson, who was noted for his films on the Arctic, to provide visual expertise. We also went down to the Press Gallery and explained what we were trying to do. Charles Lynch, then president of the Gallery, was keen on the idea.

We had, however, certain problems.

In our House of Commons, members speak from their seats, rather than a rostrum, as in the United States Congress or the United Nations. We had undertaken to provide equal visual coverage for all members, regardless of party, wherever they happened to be in the House.

Therefore, in addition to the eight cameras, we needed overhead lighting, which meant considerable heat, which meant that the House air conditioning system needed updating. All of these things were done.

Whenever the Speaker gave the floor to a member, he or she was automatically on camera. All cameras were remote-controlled in what was probably the most up-to-date control booth in the world. However, in order to conform the design of the booth to the heritage aspects of the Chamber, we brought in a special team from Public Works. It, in turn, commissioned Casavant Frères, builders for many decades of beautiful church organs, to design and construct the booth's exterior.

As word got around, a stream of visitors arrived on Parliament Hill from the European Community, the Australian Parliament, Westminster, and even the United States Congress, which had been advised to broadcast its proceedings using department store surveillance cameras. Congressman Charlie Rose of Alabama led the American delegation and I took the liberty of pointing out to him and his colleagues that the most important legislative body in the free world should have the best available broadcasting system. In the end, the United States Congress approved a resolution to broadcast its proceedings modeled on the system installed in the Canadian House of Commons—the highest recognition Canada had received from Congress since the declaration of war in 1812.

These visitors became the responsibility of Alistair Fraser, Clerk of the House, and Alexander Small, the Assistant Clerk. Jim Lansburg, one of the CBC's top engineers, played a major role in designing and creating a system that could compare favourably with the most advanced anywhere.

When Queen Elizabeth II came to open parliament, the system was up and running. However, what everyone dreaded happened. As the Speaker took his place and the camera panned along the government front bench, a prominent Liberal minister was seen industriously picking his nose.

Some self-styled experts have gone on record saying broadcasting parliament was a grave error because it permitted Canadians to see for the first time the antics, theatrics, repetition and frequent dullness of the House. I suppose the same could be said of televising baseball. The fact remains that people are watching—and the members know it.

Taxpayers have a right to the fullest information possible on the conduct of the business of the country. That means television. Certainly, Canadians know a lot more about what goes on than they did before. Question Period—whether one thinks it's a waste of time or not—has one of the largest audiences of daytime television. It can also be viewed as a re-run in the evening. The answer, therefore, is not to turn off the cameras; the answer is for the members to improve their act.

One of our first crises arose when Ralph Stewart, a prominent Liberal backbencher from Northern Ontario, decided to cross the floor to the Tories. The Grits advised the Speaker, Jim Jerome, that they did not want this episode covered. I told him if the cameras ignored this piece of political drama, the system would be shot down in flames.

We compromised.

The cameras picked up the member rising in his place, walking down to the exact centre of the Chamber, then swung to the Speaker. A few minutes later when Ralph Stewart was in his new seat, the camera swung back for a quick glimpse. Everybody was happy. The Grits because the moment of actually crossing the centre line was not shown and the Tories because the public was able to view the epochal moment when the former Grit settled in his new Tory seat.

When the Clark government went down to dismal defeat in 1980, I was working with Walter Baker, President of the Privy Council, focusing most of my attention on the House television. The day after the government's defeat, Speaker Jim Jerome renewed my contract for six months then went off to Sudbury to take up an appointment from Joe Clark as Associate Chief Justice of the Federal Court of Canada. He was in the almost unique position up to that time of having gained the trust of all parties in the House.

Under his successor, Madame Jeanne Sauvé, it was intimated to me that the television cameras which I had helped to install in the House had been at least partly responsible for the brief defeat of the Trudeau government the previous year. Recalling some of the figures on the front benches of that government, I was not surprised. It was also intimated that when my contract was up, I might gracefully retire with no hard feelings. The hitch was, according to one of the Speaker's functionaries, a number of members in both the Liberal and Conservative parties felt I was doing a good job and wanted me to stick around. In my usual co-operative way, I said I was prepared to abide by whatever decision they took.

My exact words were, "I don't give a good God-damn what you do."

I'm not proud of that language and it must be understood I used it as a vernacular expression, not as a reflection on the Deity.

Nothing happened for a while and then Pierre Trudeau decided that as his swan song, he would remodel Canada's constitution. The idea was to bring it to Canada, pass it in parliament and add a Charter of Rights and Freedoms. There were the usual roadblocks and objections from people who felt others were getting too much and they weren't getting enough.

It was my idea to televise Trudeau's Constitutional Committee. I was told to forget it; the Speaker didn't want it. I wasn't particularly concerned about Madame Sauvé's view as it was my considered opinion that Pierre Trudeau would buy it. All he needed was a little encouragement.

It had always been part of the plan to wire a number of committee rooms, such as the Railway Committee Room and a couple of rooms in the West Block, so the public could view the proceedings of important parliamentary committees. Somehow, this idea never got off the ground. Nobody could agree which committees warranted television coverage.

Therefore, my first move was to go to Erik Nielsen, Opposition House Leader, and suggest that for the benefit of all Canadians, the constitutional deliberations should be aired.

I didn't have to draw a diagram.

The next day, Nielsen was up in the House with a motion to broadcast the proceedings of the Joint Parliamentary Committee on the Constitution. To everyone's surprise, Prime Minister Trudeau expressed agreement. So that was that.

I had already arranged to have Room 200 in the West Block wired, so when I received a frantic phone call, I was able to confirm the room was ready, the cameras installed and the committee could sit whenever they wished. Canadians were able to follow the proceedings on a daily basis, and nobody could say they were left in the dark.

CHAPTER 13

Infallibility and Other Ailments

THE FIRST LAW of survival in politics is that you must appear knowledgeable. More knowledgeable, in fact, than you really are. More knowledgeable than anyone else.

Appearing knowledgeable was a specialty with Erik Nielsen, deputy prime minister in the Mulroney government. When I told Erik the *Ottawa Citizen* was running a scandalous story about Defence Minister Bob Coates, he said without blinking an eye, "I know that." When I told him the *Toronto Star* was running a scandal story about him, he merely shrugged, "I know that." Erik liked to appear as unshakeable as the icy mountains of the Yukon, from whence he hailed.

John Diefenbaker conveyed an impression of knowledgeability amounting to infallibility. Once he phoned me at home, inquiring what I was doing. When I answered that I was shingling my roof, the Chief came back, quick as a flash, "Four inches to the weather," a comment relating to the amount of shingle that should be exposed in order to obtain the best results. This was new to me, but I followed the Chief's dictum religiously and had no reason to regret it.

Allan J. MacEachen, whom I served as an adviser when he was deputy prime minister in the Trudeau government, gave an appearance of omniscience that was almost Buddhistic. MacEachen, who had the Gaelic and whose eyes became moist at the mention of Prince Charles Edward Stuart, the Young Pretender, once complimented me on my knowledge of Scottish history. Since the Feast of St Andrew's was only a few days away, I had spent some time boning up. I didn't tell him that, preferring to leave him with his illusions.

PR types, for whom public relations is a cult and a mystery through whose twisted maze they undertake to pilot naive and gullible politicians, are, of course, the supreme practitioners of the art of being knowledgeable. I cannot recall any PR person, male or female, admitting puzzlement, confusion or lack of information in front of a client and I have known a great many PR professionals, including Mel Jack, custodian of George Hees' early image; Pat MacAdam, who buffed up John Diefenbaker and later Brian Mulroney; and Bill Neville, who exercised his talents on behalf of Joe Clark and later Kim Campbell. The list is endless and in each and every case, superior knowledgeability was the qualifier.

Infallibility was never an option in my case. There were too many people in the old Parliamentary Press Gallery who knew my limitations.

Parliament brings out the best and the worst in people: good and evil, the highest and the lowest, the mediocre and the brilliant. It is a continuing study in contrasts.

In his last speech, Mackenzie King, a wielder of immense power, now a little old man huddled in his seat, apologized to the House for not entertaining the members and their wives more frequently. The costs of high office had left him in virtual penury, he claimed. When his will was probated a year later, he had left one million dollars.

The only time I saw the mighty warrior, C.D. Howe, in tears—a man who had spent more than a week in an open boat in the cold Atlantic—was when Howard Green, the Vancouver Conservative once described as "The Smiler with the Knife," attacked Howe's family in the House.

Once I was called to order by the Minister of National Defence, Brooke Claxton, who read out a piece of mine in the House, denouncing it vigorously as a trumped-up example of bad journalism. Adding to the irony was the fact that at the very moment he attacked me, I was writing radio speeches for his use at $15 a speech.

When I first went up to the Press Gallery for the *Ottawa Journal*, George Drew had just come to Ottawa as leader of the Conservative Party. He was an impressive, handsome man with a reputation as a crusading writer. He arrived in Ottawa with a solid record as Premier of Ontario, a good First World War record, a smattering of fame as the author of *Canada's Fighting Airmen*, and the man who exposed Liberal government skulduggery in the Second World War "Bren Gun Scandal," where the federal government had awarded procurement contracts to the John Inglis Company for supplying the armed services with a Czech machine-gun. Drew's charges led to a parliamentary inquiry, which more or less vindicated the King government, but added to Drew's lustre as a defender of the public weal. He had taken all of the necessary steps to position himself as the inevitable successor to the colourless John Bracken as federal Conservative leader.

Quite frankly, I liked George Drew.

Grattan O'Leary sent me out during the general election in 1949 to cover George Drew's campaign in Ontario and Quebec. I knew he admired the Conservative leader and wanted him to win. I also had a personal interest in the man's political fate. In 1945, during his last election as premier of Ontario, I conveyed to the city editor of the *Journal*—one Charles Ivers Lynch—that six French-language counties in Eastern Ontario could be Drew's for the asking if the Ontario government saw fit to present a sum of money toward the establishment of a medical school at the University of Ottawa.

"How do you know that?" Charlie asked.

I told him the information had come from an unimpeachable source. Charlie nodded. In a month or so, and just before the election, George Drew showed up at the University of Ottawa to accept a doctorate, *honoris causa*. In his acceptance speech, he announced a grant of $250,000 toward the founding of the medical school. In the following election, the Tory Party in Ontario, for the first time since Confederation, took the six French-speaking Eastern Ontario counties, which contributed to his resounding majority in the legislature. I was beginning to learn that there was more to politics than writing speeches.

I drove out to Aylmer, on the Quebec side of the Ottawa River, with George Drew one rainy night to cover a speech he was making, one of his first as Leader of the Opposition. Drew had an old roadster with a canvas top. He came out of the House in a belted trench coat and snap brim fedora, looking like Bulldog Drummond. His speech lasted for two hours and dealt with the convertibility of the pound, a subject completely over the heads of everyone present, including myself.

I was also there the night that Grattan O'Leary's son, Dillon, cut the end off George's artillery tie at a Press Gallery party. It was a nice tie, impeccably knotted in the best tradition of gunners, and Dillon snipped it with a pair of scissors. Drew laughed louder than anyone. In a crowd where he felt at ease, Drew could be a lot of fun, whereas, on a platform, he generally managed to be as remote as a man from Mars.

Diefenbaker was just the opposite. Uneasy in small groups, he could take a crowd and gather them to his bosom, make them feel that each and every one was his special concern, that he shared their griefs, miseries and, especially, their innate distrust of the Big Boys—anyone better off than they were.

Drew managed to convey the impression that he preferred the company of the Big Boys and that he wanted to be one of them, even though he was most at home with small groups.

Louis St Laurent, meanwhile, conveyed complete sincerity and concern with doing the right thing for everyone, no matter what it might cost. He was not above lecturing his hearers in a grandfatherly or Dutch Uncle manner, hence the nickname—Uncle Louis—signifying both liking and respect.

In the days before security guards and armoured limousines, Louis St Laurent was a familiar figure walking in the early evening down Elgin Street from Parliament Hill past the War Memorial, the post office, the old police station and the Lord Elgin Hotel to his apartment in the Roxborough, where George Drew also lived. It was rumoured that the prime minister and the Leader of the Opposition used to get together for a drink when the day's work was done.

* * *

I once wrote a letter to an Ottawa newspaper defending the Senate, based on the calibre of the men and women then serving in the Upper House, and got a call from the Honourable Paul Martin Sr, one of the chief ornaments of the place. He invited me to lunch at the Rideau Club to show his appreciation. Even though I was working for John Diefenbaker at the time, Paul Martin and I used to have interesting talks. He talked, I listened.

A week or so after our lunch, he called me at home and said that since he was in the area, he would drop by our house in Alymer.

I said to Shirley, "We'd better straighten the place up a bit."

"Why?"

"Somebody might drop in."

"Who, for instance?"

"You never know. Maybe Paul Martin."

"Have you flipped? Why would Paul Martin drop in?"

An hour or so later, I saw the great man's car pull up. I went out to the kitchen and said, "Shirley, Paul Martin's here."

Just as I let Paul in the living room, Shirley came storming in. When she saw Paul, she almost fainted. Paul must have wondered about the tremendous impact he seemed to have on my wife. Anyway, we had tea and cookies, and then Paul left.

*   *   *

In forty-five years on Parliament Hill, the suggestion of commissioning a psychological portrait of one's political opponent never occurred. Firstly, because the norms of psychology don't really enter in the political arena; secondly, because of a question of ethics. The notion of commissioning a psychiatric evaluation of a public figure with the clear purpose of degrading that person was foreign to any party with any pretensions to ethics or even decency. This gambit was used against Quebec Premier Lucien Bouchard by a group in the Liberal Party.

Douglas Fisher, a political observer with thirty-five years of background in practical politics and journalism on the Hill, went so far as to suggest in an *Ottawa Sun* column that Diefenbaker's opponents sometimes felt the Chief was tinctured with madness. If that were indeed the case, he was not alone in the House of Commons. It was madness some of his opponents would have liked to possess.

In John Diefenbaker's case, one could have invented a new aberration, *dementia politica*, since the Chief's approach to issues was unique, unorthodox and always effective.

The Chief never went into long-winded explanations. For example, chastising the St Laurent government for parsimony on Old Age Pensions, rather than indulging in in-depth financial tergiversations, the Chief simply referred to the Cabinet as the "Six

Buck Boys," the amount by which they had increased pensions. This made his point succinctly and with far more impact.

Then there was the case of one Lucien Rivard, a drug pedlar with alleged connections to the Liberal Party who was convicted in the United States (but not in Canada). One night he escaped from a Dade County, Florida, jail by using a garden hose to climb the wall and all Diefenbaker had to say in the 1965 election was, "It was on a night such as this that Lucien Rivard went out to water the rink," to bring the crowd to its feet.

The Chief had an uncanny ability to play a crowd as a master musician plays an organ. He pressed all the right buttons. This was a talent that mystified the Grits and would have warranted endless psychiatric speculations. The simple answer was that he knew people; all his life he had spent with ordinary citizens, as a lawyer acting in their defence, as a politician, as a participant in the kind of sidewalk debates people in small towns love to indulge in.

This is not to suggest the Chief was immune to childhood influences from which nobody is impervious, such as parental power, friendship, poverty, and so on.

In John Diefenbaker's case, his mother was the guiding power in the household. She was strong-minded, determined and generally free of illusion. Diefenbaker spent the greater part of his life attempting to live up to the ideal his mother created. Young John was going to be someone. Acting as strong counterpoint to his mother's firmness of character, underlining her uniqueness, was his rather feckless father. William Diefenbaker was an easy-going optimist, happy with his non-demanding job in the post office, reasonably content in the early days with life in a prairie homestead. Not Florence Mary Bannerman. Mrs Diefenbaker didn't hesitate to make it clear she expected something better. A lot better.

This background—strong mother, weak father—may in part help to explain John Diefenbaker's drive and determination in achieving his ambition. It doesn't explain his political strategy or his grasp of issues, which only come from experience. Just as in the case of Lucien Bouchard, psychological appraisal may indeed tell us something about the man, without explaining the tactics of the politician, which in turn derive from day-to-day activities about which no psychiatric examination tells a great deal.

There remains, of course, the overriding factor of who and what a person is underneath the layers of pride, ambition, zeal and experience. It says nothing to point out that a person in public life is ambitious or egotistical. A lot of people in private life have those same qualities. They are, in fact, common to almost everyone. Human personality is generally formed at an early age, therefore knowledge of the influences in play at that age can be revealing, assuming everyone reacts the same way when faced with similar influences—a large assumption either in public or private life.

Sean O'Sullivan was one of those rare souls who, in retrospect, must have known he would be with us only a short time and, therefore, didn't have a minute to lose in making his mark, both in politics and the church.

As a boy, he had written to the Chief and the Chief was so taken with his letter he invited him to come to lunch at the Parliamentary Restaurant.

I attended and felt rather left out of the high-level political discussion between the Chief and the twelve-year-old from Hamilton. Later, when he reached maturity, Sean ran and was elected. He distinguished his short term in the House by spearheading a bill naming the beaver as the national animal of Canada. Later, he left parliament and entered the priesthood.

Sean had ability that would have marked him out for a bishop had he lived.

After the Chief left the leadership and I was working for Allan MacEachen, Sean invited Greg Guthrie and myself to a dinner in an Ottawa hotel promoting the ineffable Paul Hellyer for the Conservative leadership. After an excellent meal and speeches lauding the man's leadership qualities to the skies, including one by Paul, Sean rose and thanked everyone for supporting Paul Hellyer for the leadership. This was something I certainly hadn't intended, nor had Guthrie, nor, I'm sure, had many of the others. This incident showed Sean's mastery of intrigue that would have taken him far in life. Hellyer, however, fizzled when he rose at the Tory convention and lashed out at "Red Tories," of whom there were quite a few present. The rumour at the time was Jack MacBeth had written that part of the speech, something he strenuously denied in the Press Club one day. He told me the lines were Paul's own.

A few years later, after a short term as a member, Sean O'Sullivan entered the priesthood and became assistant to the Bishop of Toronto. He wrote a book about the Chief in which he tended to downgrade the great man's capacities. Of course, when Sean went to work for the Chief before becoming a Member of Parliament, the Chief was in his last days. His book compared a guttering flame to a roaring conflagration, which the Chief had been in his early career.

Sean was very much in evidence at John Diefenbaker's funeral in 1979. Then, tragically, a few years later, the boy who loved politics came down with that most insidious and deadly of diseases, leukaemia. His early death cut short a brilliant career in the Church.

CHAPTER 14

One Good Turn Deserves Another

AFTER I LEFT the Leader's Office in 1970, I went home to Aylmer, Quebec, and occupied myself with good works, a fish pond, a stone wall and a tree fort for the kids.

My son Mark had a habit of bringing home animals. He once came in with a spider monkey called Sidney for his mother's birthday. Then he arrived with a large black dog, resembling the Hound of the Baskervilles. It belonged to a suicidologist, a charming man who came to visit with his wife. They decided the dog would be happier with us than tied up in the city. I built a rock garden and a house for our two ducks. When the summer was over and there was nothing more to build, I decided to go back to work.

It occurred to me that Bryce Mackasey, Minister of Labour at the time, might need a speechwriter. Bryce was your picture-book Irishman. He had a face that couldn't be anything but Irish and a walk that would have delighted anyone casting an Irish movie—slightly bent forward, arms dangling, swaying from side to side. In a business where you often run into cardboard cutouts, Bryce Mackasey is a warm, human person. Allan Phillips wrote long, philosophical dissertations for Bryce to deliver as Postmaster General and, although you could tell by the look on Bryce's face that he had no idea what his own speech was about, he never let it floor him.

Somebody once asked him: "What did you mean?"

His answer: "I don't know. I didn't read the speech. I just delivered it."

Bryce's office was in the top of a downtown tower. I went up in the elevator, saw some people I knew, got directions and walked in. Bryce was sitting by himself on a sectional couch watching the evening news. He waved me to a seat in an over-stuffed chair. There was no one else around. We watched the news together. I said I thought he might need a speechwriter. He said there might be something to the idea. He told me to see Arnie Masters, his executive assistant. Arnie sent me to see a deputy minister. We had lunch. He spent a lot of time telling me about himself.

He asked me what I would do if I was working on a speech for the minister and he wanted me to do something else? I said I would keep working on the speech for the minister. Then he asked, if there was trouble in one of the offices in Quebec and he wanted me to go down and make a report, would I be available? I said he should get someone else. I was beginning to have doubts about him.

I went back to Arnie Masters and told him the official didn't seem to be getting the full picture. I was trying to be nice. Arnie picked up the phone and told him I was coming over to sign a contract and to have it ready. I went over, but I was losing interest fast.

The deputy minister was crouched behind a large desk with a contract form in front of him. My name and relevant facts were already filled in. He paused at a box.

"I think six months will do."

"Two years."

He bit his lip.

"All right. Two years."

He named a figure.

I named a figure double that. I had seven kids and they all had healthy appetites. Plus, I had the impression this guy was playing with me. He shrugged.

"All right."

He wrote in the figure I had named and signed his name with a flourish. I picked up the contract and said, "I'll think about it." I had no intention of working for him, ever.

Next morning, I phoned and told him it was no go. That was when I called Allan MacEachen.

A few years earlier, Bryce was deeply hurt when Joe Clark fired him as chairman of Air Canada, a post to which his mentor, Pierre

Trudeau, appointed him. He had enjoyed only four months in the office when Joe called to tell him he was grounded.

Bryce was living in Lincoln, Ontario, where his mother also lived, when he got the call. As a matter of record, he was assisting at his mother's wake when he was called to the phone. It was Joe Clark with the bad news.

"Can you imagine that? I'm leading the rosary at my mother's casket when Joe calls to tell me I'm through."

Bryce ran in Lincoln in the next election and won with a majority of 708. By this time, I was working for Erik Nielsen.

Bryce was facing charges of influence peddling, which I didn't believe for a moment. Bryce demanded a parliamentary inquiry so he could be exonerated by his peers. When I heard about Bryce's trouble, I went down the hall and knocked on his door. When he saw me, his face worked with emotion.

"With friends like you, I'm not worried."

I was there because I felt he was as innocent as a newborn babe. If somebody was cozying up to him, Bryce probably thought that it was because of his charm. Besides, he was no longer a minister.

He took me into his office and we sat down. He leaned forward.

"The only person I worry about is Erik Nielsen. You know how miserable he can be."

"Don't worry about Erik."

I spoke with more confidence than I felt as I walked back to the office of the Tory Government House Leader. He was sitting behind his desk with an expression like one of the basilisks on Notre Dame in Paris; the ones that could kill with a glance.

"I've been talking to Bryce Mackasey."

"So?"

His eyes became harder and harder.

"He's in trouble."

"I know that."

There was no sympathy in Erik's glance.

"He may have made mistakes, but he isn't a crook. Anyway, you can't hit a man when he's down."

His eyes flickered. I was getting through.

"That's true."

I had broken the ice.

Erik never raised the issue. Bryce was exonerated by a committee of his peers and later by a judge, justifying my belief in his innocence.

That's not the end of the story. A couple of weeks later, I was called down to the *Toronto Star* office in the National Press Building by two reporters for whom I had a great deal of respect, Val Sears and David Vienneau.

A decade earlier, Peter Stursberg, a respected Press Gallery reporter, taped a number of people on behalf of the National Archives. Among those he taped were Greg Guthrie and myself. Another was Erik Nielsen. There were others: some in the Parliamentary Press Gallery, other members of parliament and ministers. The tapes were not for public release. Now, apparently, the *Toronto Star* had gotten hold of one Stursberg had done with Erik Nielsen. The events referred to in the Nielsen tape had taken place ten years before the tape was made, which now placed them some twenty years in the past. This didn't seem to bother the *Toronto Star*. The tape it intended to publish contained an admission by Erik Nielsen that he had listened in on the Liberal Party caucus when it was talking about him.

"What do you make of that?"

I glanced briefly at the transcript held out by Val Sears.

"What am I supposed to make of it?"

"Nielsen admits he listened in on the Liberals."

I had to laugh.

"What is that, a crime? There's no law that says you can't listen in on the Grits. I remember when half the Press Gallery used to cluster round the ventilator in the third floor washroom when the Liberal caucus was going on below in the Railway Committee Room." They had the grace to blush.

I happened to know something about the episode they were referring to. A mix-up in the wiring resulted in the deliberations of the Grit Caucus being carried by the Tory Caucus Room next door. One of those present, Alvin Hamilton, Diefenbaker's Minister of Agriculture, told me the Tories gathered round to listen to the Grits debate. It was the time of the Rivard scandal and the Liberals were talking about Erik Nielsen, who had raised the issue in the House. Rivard was a drug runner arrested in the US, with alleged connections in the Liberal Party.

I told Erik that he would be attacked in the *Star* the next morning. He assumed his usual air of omniscience on these occasions and said that he knew all about it. Even I was surprised at the headline splashed all across page one, to the effect that Nielsen admitted listening in on the Grits.

The prime minister's advisers got in on the act, offering the fatuous suggestion that Nielsen should get up and apologize to the House. Joe Clark was away at the time. I said Nielsen would be destroyed by any such stupidity. In spite of my opposition, he rose in the House and said he was sorry.

That was when the big surprise came.

Bryce Mackasey leapt to his feet on the Liberal side and went into an impassioned defence of Erik, much to the embarrassment of the Liberals. That knocked the bottom out of the *Toronto Star*'s planned demolition of a Tory who had been a thorn in the side of the Grits for many years.

Honour among thieves, you say?

I prefer to think of the ancient virtue of *noblesse oblige*, as practised by honourable parliamentarians.

INSIDE THE TENT

CHAPTER 15

Working with Allan J.

I FIRST KNEW Allan J. MacEachen when we were both summer reporters on the old *Ottawa Journal*. MacEachen was a student at St Francis Xavier University in Antigonish, Nova Scotia; I at the University of Ottawa. He liked to regale the boys on the night staff with his views on reordering society for the benefit of the dispossessed.

MacEachen soon made his mark with a full-page piece on the South March wolf hunt, south of Ottawa, complete with a six-column photo of grim-faced, heavily armed farmers and a pile of dead wolves. In the middle of the photo was Allan J. MacEachen, inscrutable even then.

Never one to play down his Scottish ancestry, MacEachen likes nothing better than to take a leading part in Scottish festivities in his native Cape Breton, or anywhere in Nova Scotia for that matter, or wherever Scottish festivities may occur. A few years ago, he appeared in kilt and sporran at the Glengarry Highland Games, in Maxville, Ontario. He even spoke in Gaelic, bringing a tear to many a Scottish eye among the Glengarrians who received their land, it must be remembered, in recognition of their loyalty to the King during the American Revolution. The Glengarrians took up arms a second time to defend Canada from the Americans in 1812.

In fact, one of Allan J. MacEachen's favourite relaxations is the pipes. MacEachen would invite a few friends and acquaintances to his Ottawa apartment after work. There, we would settle ourselves with a rum in his sitting room, while his private piper—who doubled as the minister's chauffeur—marched up and down the room, playing the bagpipes. This was no ordinary piper. He was a winner in the competitions held at Inverness, Scotland, which attracted the finest pipers in the world. It was in Inverness—from whence his mother hailed—that MacEachen first heard the piper's playing and immediately offered him a job in Canada.

These are the kind of memories among which Allan MacEachen finds himself at home.

As a member of parliament, when MacEachen came back to Ottawa, he would come out to our place in Wychwood on the Ottawa River, bringing with him a bottle of Drambuie, his preferred cordial in those days. MacEachen quite literally drank the Scotch liqueur in honour of the Young Pretender, Charles Edward Stuart. As far as MacEachen was concerned, he was no Pretender. In the imagination of Allan J. MacEachen, Bonnie Prince Charlie lives. He once threatened a friend and colleague with blackballing in the government because he had, in MacEachen's estimation, made insulting remarks about the "the Prince" at MacEachen's cottage on Lake Ainslie in Cape Breton. Hardly a place to make jokes about the Stuart Kings.

I took the trouble to do some checking on the Prince and found that in the boat that conveyed the Young Pretender to the Isle of Skye after the disaster of Culloden in 1746, there was a third person, in addition to the Prince and Flora Macdonald (the historical Flora, not the one that sat for Kingston and the Islands). That person was a Highland gillie by the name of MacEachen. As everyone knows or ought to know, a gillie is a kind of gamekeeper. When I taxed MacEachen on these facts in explanation of his obsession with the Prince, he immediately flew on the defensive.

"He was not a gillie. He was a well-known soldier-of-fortune."

Gillie or soldier-of-fortune, there he was piloting the Prince to safety, a MacEachen of the MacEachens. Nothing more remained to be said.

When I joined MacEachen in 1970, he was Minister of Manpower and Immigration. In 1972, the Liberals came back with a minority government and Prime Minister Pierre Trudeau wanted Allan MacEachen to take on the job of Government House Leader and President of the Privy Council. His friends and supporters to a man advised against what they regarded as a political demotion. I told him to grab Trudeau's offer.

"You're the only one who says that," he replied. "Everyone else tells me it's a come-down and will look bad in Cape Breton."

"Trudeau needs you. Secondly, it doesn't hurt to go along with a prime minister. They have long memories. Thirdly, you will do a hell of a job. You know the House, the procedures, the rules. Trudeau obviously wants to put on a good face in the Chamber between now and the election. He'll be grateful. And it's useful to have a grateful prime minister. Something else."

"What's that?"

"It should be easy to get the PM to boost up the Privy Council job. Make a statement saying that he is attributing new importance to the position of President of the Privy Council. You should also be able to get him to agree to letting you have a research staff."

MacEachen's eyes glistened. The former St Francis Xavier professor was still enough of an academic to be intrigued by the idea of his own research staff. It was a legitimate suggestion. The President of the Privy Council and Government House Leader is always faced with knotty problems of parliamentary jurisprudence.

I also pointed out that being Minister of Manpower and Immigration was no longer a snap.

"We'll have draft dodgers from the US this winter and high unemployment. This is a good time to get into something more positive."

MacEachen nodded.

"You've convinced me."

I realized I had persuaded him to go the way he wanted to go.

As I was leaving the office, he cleared his throat.

"I'd like you to come over with me to the Privy Council."

I agreed. I didn't relish the idea of floating around in the bureaucracy for another year. Manpower was fast losing its charm. However, when I got to the Privy Council with MacEachen, I encountered a veritable forest of raised eyebrows. What was a known Tory, a man who had worked for Diefenbaker, doing with the House Leader of the Liberal Party? Some people went so far as to question me on this issue. I had to laugh.

MacEachen got his research staff and we crowded them into the top floors of the Varette Building on Slater Street. They beavered away on a major report on the parliamentary committee system, which I assumed meant attending a lot of committee meetings. They informed me that there was no question of actually attending committees. The procedure was to read up on everything written about the committee system by previous academic researchers. When the report came out, MacEachen refused to accept it. Bill MacEachern, Allan J.'s executive assistant, was scathing in his criticism. I made allowances for the rarefied atmosphere in which the researchers worked and damned it with faint praise.

One noted academic said to me, "I don't understand why the minister keeps you around."

I had been waiting for the question.

"To keep idiots like you from getting him into trouble."

MacEachen did a fine job as Government House Leader. I tried to interest him in putting cameras in the House of Commons, but to no avail. He felt that the result would reduce parliament to entertainment. Perhaps he was right. Anyway, I went ahead and prepared a cabinet document on the issue.

MacEachen concentrated on his job as House Leader in a minority government with occasional lapses when the Scottish heritage was imperiled.

The CBC was running a Gaelic-language program in Halifax. Somebody got the bright idea to cancel it, which brought MacEachen immediately into the fray. The issue was raised before the Broadcasting Committee, whose chairman was James Jerome, later Speaker of the House. Bob Muir, MP for Cape Breton-The Sydneys, a former coal miner, stood up day after day before the committee, insisting that the Gaelic-language program remain on air.

Every day MacEachen would ask: "How's Bob Muir doing? Is he putting up a fight?"

"A powerful battle, Minister. Muir is a tower of strength."

MacEachen, whose father was a Cape Breton coal miner, would rub his hands with glee. The fact that Muir was a Tory didn't enter into the equation and I had the impression that MacEachen was busily pulling strings in the background to give Muir all the help he could.

I had once seen Muir flatten an anti-Diefenbaker protester in the Château Laurier without turning his head or missing his stride. After de Gaulle made his famous "Vive le Québec libre!" intervention on a Montreal balcony, Muir made a speech demanding freedom for Bretons in France. He received hundreds of letters and dozens of invitations to speak in Brittany. However, since he didn't speak French, he had to turn them down.

Bob Muir had been seriously injured in a coal mine accident and, in the late '70s, his pain was such that he considered resigning his seat in the House. He got a call from Allan J. MacEachen, then Deputy Prime Minister, offering him a Senate appointment. The sharpies in the Tory party told Muir to turn down the offer. It was a case of the Liberals trying to get Muir's seat, they said. I remembered MacEachen's reaction when Muir was fighting for the Gaelic. I said Allan J. was sincere. I advised him to grab the Senate appointment. After all, he was the one who was suffering. He took the seat and became a force in the Senate. The NDP, by the way, got the riding.

As Minority House Leader, MacEachen's skill saved the Trudeau government half a dozen times until, in 1974, the Liberals regained their majority. Trudeau rewarded MacEachen by naming him Minister of External Affairs, an area where I couldn't be of much help. I stayed with the Privy Council until Mitchell Sharp came in and grabbed on to the television proposal, which I happily helped implement.

* * *

The Chief didn't know it, but it was through Allan MacEachen's personal intervention that the Government of Canada granted consent for John Diefenbaker to receive the Companion of Honour from the hands of Her Majesty the Queen.

Her Majesty felt it would be appropriate to recognize John Diefenbaker for his years of unswerving loyalty. However, in order for the Chief to accept the honour, the Canadian government would have to approve. When I mentioned the dilemma, MacEachen went to work. It might be stretching it a bit to suggest that MacEachen's enthusiasm had anything to do with the fact that Diefenbaker's ancestors on his mother's side, the Bannermans, sprang from Inverness, Scotland, also the stamping grounds of MacEachen's forebears.

It is a fact that ties of Scottish kinship, like underground wiring, foster mutual recognition among those of Highland descent. This may indeed explain the Scottish peculiarities of soberness and pawkiness, which are such a part of the Canadian character. In fact, Flora MacDonald (the modern one) once said there were more Gaelic-speaking ministers in John A. Macdonald's government than there were English or French. Suffice to say that the Trudeau government granted full approval to the acceptance by John Diefenbaker of the Queen's high honour. No one was happier than Allan J. MacEachen.

Paul Martin Sr, Canadian High Commissioner, met the Chief on his arrival in London in full panoply. He was visibly basking in his own recent induction to the Order of Canada. At the press conference called by Paul Martin, the Chief dwelt at some length on the historic importance of the Companion of the Honour, received from the hands of Her Majesty, in comparison with lesser awards, such as the Order of Canada. Paul bore up manfully, knowing the Chief as he did.

* * *

In earlier days, MacEachen leaned toward re-constituting society according to socialistic principles. One night during the 1960s, in the Belle Claire Hotel in Ottawa, I joined T. Ainslie Kerr, reporter at the *Ottawa Journal* and graduate of St Francis Xavier, and Allan J. MacEachen, former professor at St F.X. and later assistant to Prime Minister Lester B. Pearson, for a libation. We met at MacEachen's invitation in the room of Clairie Gillis, CCF member for Cape Breton South. The CCF was the forerunner of the NDP. Clairie, a coal miner by trade, had lately distinguished himself by punching out a waiter in a local hotel—not the Belle Claire. It was his inviolable principle never to punch out a waiter where he was staying.

An MP punching out a waiter is definitely in the man-bites-dog news category and Clairie found himself in the headlines. MacEachen, also a Cape Bretoner and a coal miner's son, could sympathize with Clairie. Ainslie, with his St F.X. background and Scots blood, was very much in tune with the other two. I was the odd man out, a combination of stolid Dutch and mercurial Irish, constantly at odds with my own psyche. That night in the old Belle Claire, we settled many of the outstanding problems of the nation. In the days when he was taking a drink, Allan J. MacEachen was quite a jovial person. It was only when he reached ministerial status and gave up rum and Drambuie that the dourness of his Highland ancestry took over.

Not long ago on a visit to our home, MacEachen revealed he had taken a vacation in the lonely northern Hebrides and felt completely at home among the barren hills and crashing sea.

"I was very well treated."

"Were you well treated as a widely-known Canadian, or because you were a MacEachen of the MacEachens?"

"Because I was a MacEachen, of course."

* * *

Judy LaMarsh once described Allan MacEachen as the "laziest man in Cabinet," a misnomer, if ever there was one.

The charge derived from MacEachen's attitude of unflappable insouciance. I worked for MacEachen for four years after I left Stanfield's office and while his pace was not mercurial, it was steady, deliberate and constructive. Without panic or flap, MacEachen coolly and systematically got things done.

This was certainly true when Trudeau flirted with retirement during the Clark government's brief, but disastrous, tenure. MacEachen firmly believed the Clark government, which seemed to be afflicted with a kind of purposeful lethargy, could be defeated. He didn't want John Turner or Donald McDonald to reap the benefit. He also maintained that the only Liberal capable of bringing the party back to the seats of the mighty, from which it had been so rudely ejected, was Pierre Elliott Trudeau.

Joe's government went down to defeat on the Crosbie budget.

Once again, to nobody's great astonishment, there was Pierre Trudeau, centre stage, in a puff of smoke, smiling, bowing and pirouetting, thoughts of retirement all forgotten. Away went the leadership convention, whisked away on the winds of chance, leaving John Turner, the Liberal Party's Sir Galahad, and Donald McDonald, its Friar Tuck, on the sidelines, wondering what hit them.

And smiling in the background like a Cheshire cat was MacEachen, purring with pleasure at the turn of events he had so artfully arranged.

The Clark Tories hurled themselves vigorously into the job of losing the election. They fanned out across the country, desperately trying to persuade bemused voters they would improve their lot by voting for an increase in the price of gasoline. All indications showed this argument was falling on deaf ears.

Joe Clark and his government were out after one of the shortest tenures in Canadian history.

Once again, Pierre Trudeau was prime minister.

Allan MacEachen, for his efforts, received the unrewarding job of Finance Minister and had to wait two years for the one he really coveted, External Affairs.

CHAPTER 16

The Man from the Yukon

THE PHONE rang and it was Erik Nielsen.
"What are you doing?"
"Nothing."

It wasn't quite true. I was at home in Russell, Ontario, by the banks of the Castor, working on a novel about the War of 1812. I had done a lot of research on the event, a conflict between British North America and the United States, which we won. I had read letters and documents from the era, written by people who participated; in fact, I had virtually withdrawn to 1812. I spent my days with Sir Isaac Brock, Tecumseh, Red George Macdonnell, and other heroes of the time. However, I discovered on enquiry, that if there is one plot no Canadian publisher is interested in, it's a novel set during the War of 1812.

So, I set aside this monumental work to go into the House of Commons and work for Erik, who had just been appointed Opposition House Leader by Joe Clark. It was near the end of that disastrous winter of 1980, where the Tories had been defeated in a national election ending Joe's nine-month term as prime minister.

I think it was Dick Jackson, city editor of the *Ottawa Journal*, who described Erik Nielsen as "The White Wolf of the Yukon." Erik came to Ottawa in the first Diefenbaker government, a young Yukon lawyer, bush flyer, and decorated Second World War fighter pilot. After the defeat of the Tories in 1963, Erik turned his full attention on the Liberals. His probing in the Rivard Case, involving a suspected drug peddler with connections in the office of Guy Favreau, Minister of

Justice, gave rise to a Commission of Inquiry and resulted in the resignation of Pearson's parliamentary secretary and the conviction of an assistant to the Minister of Citizenship and Immigration. Nielsen's probing earned him the undying hatred of the Liberal hierarchy. He became a *bête noire*, a kind of Robespierre who must be dealt with.

The stigma even attached to those working with him. A little while after I joined Erik, a Liberal friend told me there was unhappiness in high places about my working for Nielsen.

"Watch yourself. They're out to get you."

I laughed. I could take care of myself.

About a month before the federal election in 1984, when I was still in Erik's office, I received notice of a taxation reassessment going back five years and informing me that I owed something like $20,000. Had they waited a couple of months, the five-year term beyond which reassessment cannot take place would have been up. They got in just under the wire. After the election, when I had moved to the PMO, I went down to see the official in charge of my case. I was under considerable restraint because I was now working for the prime minister. I knew and he knew that I would have to pay. My only other option was to take the case to court; and this was not the kind of publicity I wanted to visit on the prime minister.

I pointed out that they had previously reassessed me on each and every year that they were now, again, reassessing. I showed them their own print-outs where my assessments had been altered in accordance with their adjustments. In effect, they were reassessing their own reassessments. Anyone who has ever argued with anyone at Revenue Canada knows what it is like to beat your head against a stone wall.

The answer the official gave me was that he could not be held responsible for reassessments performed by a clerk in the office. I found that a curious reply indeed. We were operating under rules made by his department and he was telling me he wasn't accepting responsibility.

The major reassessment involved an office I had built for myself through a contractor in anticipation of leaving government and going into business for myself. In that year, I had described myself as a writer. Apparently, that designation sends off all kinds of signals in the bureaucratic mind. The official told me a writer could have no expectation of a reasonable profit and, therefore, could not deduct such things as office space, typewriter, desk, and filing cabinets. I pointed out that if I went into business as a meat-cutter and built myself a shop, those expenses would be deductible. He agreed, but said that a meat-cutter had reasonable expectations of profit. The fact that I had made $60,000 (and paid tax on it) as a freelance speech writer did not even register. A writer just cannot make money and, therefore, should not build himself working space in his home. The interview ended when I said it was now quite clear to me why Canadian writers, artists, dramatists and entertainers were leaving the country to work in the United States or England. They were being driven out by Revenue Canada officials who do not possess the slightest inkling of what creativity is about.

I don't want this to sound like sour grapes (whatever they sound like). The fact is, just about this time, writers and artists stormed parliament demanding a change in tax laws, whereby they received less consideration than plumbers. Promises were made. Nothing much has changed.

I originally told Erik that I would work for three days a week as I had no desire to get back on the fly paper. He had agreed with suspicious alacrity and, within a few months, I was back on the old schedule, six days a week and evenings.

Erik had a nice, big office in the East Block, which I was privileged to share. There, I scanned the daily media and prepared notes for the House. I went in a couple of times a day to chat with Erik, where we would discuss the issues and problems of the day. Erik's brother, Leslie, the Hollywood star, sometimes came to visit and we would take him over to the National Press Club where he amused the members at the bar with a whoopee cushion. His motto: Anything for a laugh.

The first issue I raised with Erik was the generally moribund posture of the Official Opposition in the House. This made Erik angry.

"What do you mean? I think we're looking good. We're showing up well in Question Period."

"Off the Hill, the Official Opposition might as well be dead."

In fact, there were people on Parliament Hill who didn't have the slightest idea what was going on. Most of the information getting through the media screen to the public was slanted towards the government, which was natural. After all, the Liberals had just won an election the Tories had been stupid enough to lose.

"So, what do you want us to do?" he asked.

Erik was becoming irritated at my persistence.

"Raise hell. Do something that proves the Tory Party lives."

I pointed out that the Trudeau government was bringing in a massive omnibus bill, incorporating a number of other bills. I said this was undemocratic. As Erik Nielsen pointed out in his book, *The House is not a Home*, the National Energy Policy of the Liberal government in 1980 was embodied in the Omnibus Bill, which, in fact, incorporated nineteen separate bills, depriving elected members of their right to vote on each separate issue. I suggested that the Tories should refuse to vote on the bill as a protest against the infringement of democratic rights.

Erik thought that would constitute a childish gesture.

I shrugged and took off for Barbados to relax on the beach.

I was doing exactly that, sipping rum punch and watching the lime-green sea, when I caught a piece of news on the radio to the effect that the Conservative Opposition had walked out of parliament to protest a government omnibus bill. The bells calling members in to the House had been ringing frantically for several days. I thought, what have I done? We could go to the Tower for this. When I came back to Ottawa ten days later, I couldn't believe my ears. The bells were ringing frantically in the corridors of the East Block, and every other building on the Hill. I found Erik seated behind his desk, looking complacent.

"I didn't expect you to go on this long."

His look became smug.

"When I start something, I carry on to the end."

The Tories marched into the House a few days later, having made a point that resounded across the country: the Conservative Party lived.

Erik never wavered in his loyalty to Joe Clark. While I was impressed, I wondered if there was something more than just loyalty to the leader. While Joe had many fine qualities, he was no Diefenbaker in my book. I asked Erik what the secret was. He sat back and gave me his bomber pilot look.

"I went to school in Smoky Lake, Alberta."

I found this piece of information interesting—Erik's father had been stationed at the RCMP detachment there—but irrelevant. I had been to Smoky Lake in the 1958 campaign with the then Labour Minister, Mike Starr. When Mike began speaking in Ukrainian, people wept in the back of the hall. Driving into Smoky Lake was like driving into a village in Ukraine. There was the onion tower on the church, the dark pines and spruce lining the road, the huddle of homes under a lowering sky. At a meeting in the school, the men wore leather or sheepskin jackets and heavy pants tucked in the tops of gum-rubber boots. In somebody's kitchen, we sat drinking rye and water out of white china cups and everyone spoke Ukrainian, except myself. I wished some of my Quebec friends could have been there to get a down-to-earth glimpse of Anglo-Canadian culture.

"So, you went to school in Smoky Lake."

"Be patient. Soon, you will know all. My teacher was the lady who later became Joe's mother."

He sat back as though that settled everything.

"What are you saying. That you and Joe are related?"

"Don't be silly."

He assumed a pained expression.

"So, you back Joe to the limit simply because his mother taught you in school."

This conversation took place at a time when Brian Mulroney's supporters were pulling out all the stops to replace Joe with Brian. Every morning in the West Block cafeteria, a little group of Mulroney men talked up his leadership with the media. And, if there was ever a time for the ambitious Quebec Irishman—bilingual as Trudeau—it was now. However, Erik's expression told me that the subject was closed. As far as he was concerned, there was only one leader—Joe Clark.

I went to England with Erik and his new wife to represent the party at a World Conservative Conference. Erik, whose first wife died under tragic circumstances, had recently married Shelley, an attractive member of the House of Commons security staff. The wedding took place in Bermuda at the home of Sir William Stephenson, the wartime spymaster popularly known as "The Man Called Intrepid," who gave the bride away.

The World Conservative Conference was a prestigious affair. Margaret Thatcher spoke at the luncheon, followed by Jacques

Chirac, Mayor of Paris; George Bush, Vice President of the United States; Helmut Kohl, Chancellor of West Germany; Kakuei Tanaka, former Prime Minister of Japan; and half a dozen others. I found out Erik was on the list to speak for the Progressive Conservative Party of Canada. I quickly managed to borrow a large, old-fashioned Underwood from Captain Peter John, Margaret Thatcher's security chief. I set it up on the table where the media reception was being held and Captain John, a hard-bitten six-footer, swept aside the canapés. I typed up notes for Erik Nielsen while members of the world press leaned over my shoulder and offered helpful suggestions. Erik's hors d'oeuvres speech won rounds of applause.

Captain John, who had been in charge of security for an Arab emir, gave me some tips on protecting the famous. He recommended the Canadian-made, eight-shot Browning automatic as a useful weapon in a tight fix. It never misfires.

"Thanks. I'll keep that in mind," I replied.

Afterwards, I went out and stood on the steps of the Intercontinental Hotel, at Hyde Park and Piccadilly. A very large police inspector took up a position on the sidewalk. Across the street, people were waving placards denouncing Prime Minister Margaret Thatcher and the general state of the universe. The police inspector gave me permission to stay where I was, provided I didn't cause any trouble. In a few minutes, a Jaguar pulled up and out stepped Mrs Thatcher, so close that I had to back out of the way. I had expected a large, Boadicea-like woman. Instead, she appeared rather slight and quite attractive, with red-gold hair.

If I said she gave me a big smile, some people would think I was lying; but that's exactly what she did. She must have taken me for a plain clothes policeman. An Inspector, probably. I bowed politely as she went inside.

A few minutes later, I passed George and Barbara Bush crossing the lobby. They looked like a nice, average American couple. I said, "Good morning," and got a cheery response. I dropped in to the vice president's press conference where the US marine guard at the door had the most beautiful shoe-shine I have ever seen. Bush handled himself smoothly and expertly with the British and American press. I was impressed to find that, in England, the print medium has pride of place. The boys with their mikes poised for "sound bites" stand at the back of the room. The *Times*, *Guardian*, *Express*, *Telegraph* and other moulders of public opinion are front and centre. They ask the questions.

Bush wound up his speech with the pledge that "Government of the people, by the people and for the people shall not perish." He didn't bother to credit Abraham Lincoln. Perhaps it wasn't needed.

Later, there was a cocktail party on the fourth floor overlooking Hyde Park. Nielsen spent a lot of time gazing absently out the window.

"Last time I was here, I was flying over in a Mosquito bomber."

Erik was always a fun guy.

CHAPTER 17

Joe Clark — "Look: No Hands!"

I REMEMBER a gangling kid named Joe Clark who dropped off press releases in the Chief's Parliament Hill office. Joe was working at Tory Party headquarters under the National Director, Dalton Camp, and the Party Secretary, Flora MacDonald, both of whom were industriously working to oust John Diefenbaker as leader.

A dozen years later at the 1976 leadership convention, which I attended with John Diefenbaker, Joe Clark emerged as leader of the party, beating out a Quebec candidate called Brian Mulroney for the job.

The Chief favoured Claude Wagner, a former Quebec Justice Minister, but I had doubts about him. He wore lifts on his heels.

Then, in the 1979 election, the impossible happened.

Joe Clark, the improbable candidate, emerged as prime minister with a minority government, beating out Pierre Trudeau, who seemed to have completely lost interest in politics.

As prime minister, Joe Clark—age forty—demonstrated a tendency to embrace not only the unpredictable, but the unbelievable. At the outset, although he headed a minority government, Joe promised to govern as though he had a majority. That placed Joe in the category of a bird flying with one wing. Like Icarus, who in mythic times flew over the Aegean on giant wings held on with wax, Joe held up until the melt-down, which came nine months later.

The Liberals, stunned by the reversal of fortune, began making plans to redress the blip called Joe Clark.

I was reclining in my favourite spot—the golden sands of Barbados—when I learned that Pierre Trudeau had taken a walk in the snow and decided to resign as Liberal leader. John Turner, relaxing on the beach in Jamaica, announced he wanted Trudeau's job. These were the first moves that launched an exercise in political dynamics.

In the unfolding series of events that brought the Clark government crashing down, restored Pierre Trudeau to power, cut out John Turner and Donald MacDonald, I sensed the guiding hand of Allan Joseph MacEachen. Compared to the Cape Breton guru, Machiavelli was a rank amateur.

Political dynamics, as distinguished from text book politics, requires a political brain to move pieces about on a chess board to achieve desired results. All of the pieces must move at precisely the right time in the right direction in order to be successful. Political dynamics uses one piece to cancel another. It worries little about such mundane activities as speech making or baby kissing. Instead, it thinks in terms of corruption and regeneration, to use an Aristotelian concept.

MacEachen was a master of this kind of contriving. Perhaps conniving would be a better word.

To the people around Joe Clark, the world of parliament—electoral strategy, political psychology, the things that turn failure into victory—remained a closed book. In rodeo terms, what happened to the Clark government might be compared to "hazing calves into the chute." Having hazed the opposition into the chute, you rope and brand them.

The Clark government, having had the life-span of a fetus in gestation, died stillborn.

Joe spent much of his time in the West, holding Cabinet meetings in resort areas, emerging from time to time with policy declarations patched together around the pool.

This was not a sound posture with a political craftsman like Allan J. MacEachen sitting in the wings. Behind MacEachen, waiting for his call, Pierre Trudeau stood pirouetting.

Marc Lalonde, then Trudeau's assistant, took on the task of persuading the Quebec members that only Trudeau could save the day and return the Liberals to power. Lalonde's eloquence and a bit of arm-twisting persuaded them it was time to forgive Trudeau for losing the election.

The plan, formulated by MacEachen with Marc Lalonde and, later, Trudeau, Jean Chrétien and other loyal Grits, called for three steps. In essence, success depended on none of those targeted being aware of what was happening until too late.

First, the House would become the abattoir, where the stumbling Clark government would be felled like a pole-axed ox. Governments defeated in the House were inevitably defeated in the subsequent election.

Second, Trudeau would have to be persuaded to reconsider and resume his position at the helm of the party, at least for the election. Later, he could do as he saw fit.

Third, under Trudeau's restored and brilliant leadership, the Grits would clobber the upstart Tories in the election, restoring Liberal party rule, without which the country would inevitably founder.

For the agile minds of Trudeau and MacEachen, not to mention Lalonde, none of the above presented any great difficulties. Once Trudeau agreed to participate, the rest was simple.

Neither John Turner nor Donald McDonald was consulted on the strategy, as the Trudeau Old Guard neither liked nor trusted either. Both were regarded as closet Tories.

The foolproof plan had the advantage not only of getting rid of the Tory government and re-electing the Grits, but also eliminating the two contenders unacceptable to the Liberal hierarchy, Turner and McDonald.

Through the Parliament Hill jungle came intimations of activity, just as in a natural jungle, scents and sounds are carried on the breeze. Rumours of plots and schemes swirled around furtive meetings of denizens gathered at the watering holes—the Parliamentary Restaurant, the Confederation Building Dining Room, the West and Centre Block cafeterias. From many sources came whispers of Grit action to topple the Clark government. Joe's vulnerability stood out a mile; you had to be either asleep or indifferent not to see it.

The Clark government, bewitched by the euphoria of power, couldn't believe the Grits would dare engineer a House defeat (which they could easily do with the co-operation of their friends in the NDP). Or, even if they did succeed in defeating the government, that they could go on to win the election. Joe Clark and his advisers were convinced that if an election came, they would win.

That misguided belief was shattered by the budget brought down by the Minister of Finance, John Crosbie.

MacEachen himself could not have crafted a better instrument to destroy a government. Although responsible and fiscally sound, the budget handed the Liberals a dagger, handle first—an eighteen-cent-a-gallon increase in the price of gasoline.

To anyone on Parliament Hill at the time, it was clear that the Liberals intended to pull the plug on the Clark government using the Crosbie budget as provocation. I told Erik Nielsen, Government House Leader, the night before the vote that the government would go down on the budget. He shrugged.

"They wouldn't dare."

Another Tory friend of mine said, "I hope they defeat us in the House, because we will then sweep the country."

All the optimism seemed to me misplaced. I happened to know that no government defeated in the House has ever come back to win the election brought on by its defeat.

And thus it happened, on December 13, 1979, exactly according to MacEachen's plan.

Defeated in the House and forced to go to the country, the Clark Tories entered an election on the issue of an eighteen-cent-a-gallon tax increase on gasoline. I even found people around Joe Clark who felt Canadians would vote for the gasoline price increase because it made sound fiscal sense. Usually when people vote, one of their least visible motivations is one based on sound fiscal sense.

As the election staggered to its inevitable close, strange reports started coming in from the Middle East about Americans finding asylum from mob violence in the Canadian Embassy in Teheran, due to the courage of the Canadian ambassador to Iran, Ken Taylor. He had risked his own safety to smuggle Americans out of the country, using Canadian passports, and away from mob action by the followers of the Ayatollah Khomeini, the modern version of the Mad Mullah.

The situation became tense when a Canadian Press Gallery reporter got wind of the story and began making pointed inquiries and clearly suggesting that he was prepared to publish the story. Taylor managed to secure a promise that the story would not be broken until the last American left the Canadian embassy.

When the Americans had been liberated from the Ayatollah's grasp, I pointed out to Lowell Murray, who was handling strategy for Joe Clark, that Ambassador Taylor's heroic behaviour was a hell of a lot more marketable than a rise in the price of gasoline. The government should have been moving to take credit for the action of their representative in Teheran. My feeling was that if the Clark government stopped talking about the budget and used the episode in Iran instead, they might have been able to pin the campaign on something positive. Nothing happened until the last week of the campaign when Flora MacDonald, the minister responsible, gave a reluctant and obligatory bow in the direction of Ambassador Taylor.

It was, of course, too little, too late.

The Clark government went down to crashing defeat, brought on by its own ineptness, false confidence and Grit skulduggery.

When the dust and smoke cleared away—presto! chango!—Pierre Trudeau was once again centre stage, smiling and pirouetting, thoughts of retirement gone up in a puff of smoke.

Joe Clark and his government were out after one of the shortest terms in Canadian history. It took John Turner to outdo Joe Clark. Clark had nine months in office; Turner, four. Both paled by comparison with the four days in office enjoyed by Arthur Meighen during the 1925 Constitutional Crisis.

One person viewed the dismal Tory performance with more than ordinary interest. Brian Mulroney, a perfectly bilingual Montreal labour lawyer, had grown up in Baie Comeau, a Quebec paper mill town, attended St Francis Xavier and Laval Universities and won recognition as counsel for the Cliche Commission on labour violence. Mulroney had never accepted the 1976 convention verdict that awarded Joe Clark leadership of the Tory Party. He nourished a deep conviction he could do better—a hell of a lot better. Now, he prepared to move.

Many have criticized Mulroney's tactics in wresting the leadership away from Joe. However, he couldn't have done it without Joe's help. Joe seemed to be completely at the mercy of events, wrapped in fatalistic determinism. Mulroney was convinced he could take the party to victory, and Joe couldn't. It was, therefore, his duty to do so.

A lot of people were surprised when Joe Clark, after getting the support of 66.9 per cent of the delegates at the Winnipeg leadership review in February 1983, called for a leadership convention. This appeared to be another case of Joe's advisors taking too much for granted. If you get 66.9 per cent, without any opposing candidates, the chances are you will drop down if you enter a contest against candidates who have a degree of credibility.

I went to the leadership convention at steamy Lansdowne Park in Ottawa that July day in 1983 and met Jack Horner, former Member of Parliament for Broken Head, Alberta, and now chairman of the Canadian National Railways, appointed by Trudeau. Jack entertained us in the Chairman's Suite at the Château Laurier in his stocking feet. Jack told me by exactly how much Mulroney would win the convention. He was right on.

Erik Nielsen, on the other hand, was pushing for Joe.

He entertained a group of provincial premiers at a downtown Ottawa hotel. I was in the kitchen making drinks. I knew quite a few of the premiers. I had written speeches for John Buchanan of Nova Scotia and had gotten to know Bill Davis of Ontario pretty well when I was with the Chief. I knew most of the others at least by sight and name. When I came in with drinks, I was greeted as a friend.

Joe's problem was that he failed to assess the disillusion in his own party. A lot of Tories were annoyed with Joe because he had failed to rid the country of Pierre Elliott Trudeau. Trudeau was back, more irritating than ever, pirouetting in the very presence of Her Majesty and more than a little boring with his endless constitutional preoccupations and his harping on bilingualism. A substantial segment of the voters wanted all that gone.

And Joe was buying it all. Buying patriation of a constitution that had been drawn up in Canada in the first place. Buying a Charter of Rights that granted protection to minority rights in every province but one—the only one where French was not the minority language. There were dimly felt but powerful unseen pressures undercutting Joe's security.

Brian Mulroney's position was clear. Clark had had his chance. Now, let someone take it on who could do a better job. Brian Mulroney felt he was that man. Although he and Joe Clark were friends—hovering on the Red Tory fringe—Mulroney was the first to admit there was no room for friendship in politics.

"It's this way, Brian . . ." Tom Van Dusen advising Prime Minister Brian Mulroney on the hidden political landmines which abound on Parliament Hill.

Some of the tactics employed by Mulroney and his managers probably hurt Mulroney more than Clark. Stories of down-and-outs from homeless shelters signed on as delegates didn't sit well. Curiously, Mulroney was picking up support in caucus and from among western members, where Joe should have been strongest.

Nowhere in anyone's political Bible does it say it is wrong to aspire to party leadership, or campaign towards that objective when a party leader is faltering or tagged a loser, as was the case with Joe. His course had been one of backing and filling; his policies tentative and uninspired; his personality tepid, at best. An innate honesty and decency compensated for his failings which were, after all, rectifiable by time.

There were no visible tears, as I recall, when Lester Pearson went down to Quebec City to tell Louis St Laurent he was through.

In all candour, however, it must be admitted the Liberals do these things better, with a *savoir faire* that comes with long-time immersion in power.

The Mulroney campaign, however, went after the leadership with all the delicacy of a bull moose in the rutting season. Joe's store-bought leadership was slipping away. Who would inherit? Flora MacDonald? John Crosbie? Sinc Stevens? Mulroney and his supporters made up their minds that it would be Brian Mulroney. And they succeeded.

Brian Mulroney came into the fourth-floor office of the Opposition Leader after the convention. I had seen him rarely since the days when I worked in the very same office for John Diefenbaker, seventeen years earlier. He had grown older, experienced, wiser—but the grin was still there.

"I thought I might find you here," he said.

Brian asked me to stay on in the office once occupied by the Chief. Joe Clark moved out, a simple backbencher once more. Meanwhile, Brian Mulroney began to get ready for the election.

CHAPTER *18*

Pierre Trudeau—A Man for All Seasons

I HAVE ALWAYS felt a sneaking admiration for Pierre Trudeau, the most intellectual of our prime ministers. I admire his capacity to rise to the occasion—an important quality in politics—his readiness to deal positively with problems and, of course, his wit.

In 1990, at a *Maclean's* magazine reception in Ottawa, my daughter Lisa brought me across to say hello to the former prime minister. Trudeau wasted no time getting a shot off.

"But your father is a big Tory."

"I always suspected, Prime Minister, that you were a Conservative at heart."

"I am. A John A. Macdonald Conservative."

I could buy that.

Trudeau is a Quebec aristocrat to his fingertips. Even his mastery of French leaves no doubt about his antecedents.

The French Revolution—that great leveller of the classes—never reached Quebec. There are still two distinct classes in the province: the *petite aristocratie* of Quebec and the mass of workers, farmers and plain ordinary people who have always been regarded as beneath the class of notaries, doctors, priests and teachers.

I once went into a Quebec doctor's office in gum-rubber boots and an old mackinaw, and found myself, rather to my surprise, being ordered about like a menial. When I suddenly switched from French to English, the doctor became a model of politeness and suavity. He had one attitude when he thought that I was a member of Quebec's lower class and another when he discovered that I was an Anglo. These are the people who believe in the separatist dream.

Quebec society is collective, as society was in France before the Revolution in 1789. That is, when an idea catches hold, everyone tends to move in the same direction. This is contrary to individualistic Anglo-Saxon society where each tends to go his own way, unless and until general consensus can be reached. A movement to separate Ontario from the rest of Canada would never make headway, first, because being against the best interests of the people of Ontario, it would gain no support; and second, because individual self-interest would reject the idea.

Pierre Trudeau possesses something of the individualism of the Anglo-Saxon, although he is a Quebecker through and through. I first saw the man in a television interview when he was still virtually unknown outside Quebec. He spoke impeccable English and it took a few moments before I realized that this was the dashing editor of *Cité Libre* who had called Lester Pearson "the unfrocked priest of peace" when he allowed the United States to place atomic weapons on Canadian soil.

I should have known. The monkish face, tight-cut hair, unaccented English—it had to be Pierre Trudeau, the Quebec scholar who had fought the Duplessis government over the violent asbestos strike, visiting the site to encourage the embattled workers, and had written books about Canada and the constitution. The bright, hard edge of the man shone clearly through the fuzzy TV screen, revealing complete confidence in his ability to resolve any situation through sheer intellectual power. There was no question he had the gift. However, his weakness came out later: a tendency to apply abstract principles to human situations. Risky in any field, dangerous in politics.

Two years later, he was Minister of Justice in the Pearson government—his intemperate outburst against Pearson forgiven, if not forgotten—personally taking on Quebec Premier Daniel Johnson at the televised Confederation of Tomorrow conference. Trudeau was the star of the show, and it proved to be his launching pad to the leadership of the Liberal Party and, ultimately, Canada.

Trudeau was aware of the possibilities of pent-up violence in Quebec society and moved quickly and surely to counter them. At the

St Jean Baptiste parade in Montreal on the eve of the 1968 general election, he became the target of a hostile demonstration, but refused to leave the platform. Viewed on television, Trudeau's courage won thousands of votes.

Trudeau also endeared himself to voters in English-speaking Canada by showing clearly he had no time for the fantasies of the Quebec separatists. He was against special rights or privileges for Quebec. He felt segregating Quebec from the other provinces was simply separation on the instalment plan. A separate, isolated Quebec would wither away, a linguistic enclave in the North American English sea. So, when violence associated with a separate Quebec broke out in the '70s, Trudeau moved immediately.

On the night of October 16, 1970, I sat in the House while Trudeau revived the *War Measures Act* at the request of the Government of Quebec, giving the federal government the power to arrest without charges and to hold suspects at the Queen's pleasure, just as Louis St Laurent had done in the Gouzenko case. Although debate see-sawed back and forth, there was, in fact, little real opposition to Trudeau's demand for emergency powers. *Le Front de Liberation du Québec*—the FLQ—had viciously and brutally murdered Pierre Laporte, Quebec Minister of Labour, before stuffing his body in the trunk of a car left at Dorval Airport in Montreal. They also kidnapped British diplomat James Cross, snatching him from his Montreal home while he played on the lawn with his children. People couldn't believe this was happening in Canada and not some backward banana republic.

Trudeau clamped down, even to the extent of calling in the armed forces. In so doing, he went against the advice of the federal Minister of Justice, John Turner. Trudeau thought he knew Quebec and its potential for violence better than Turner. He had the backing of Gerard Pelletier and Jean Marchand, who also knew Quebec as well as he did.

These events did not occur in a vacuum. The country had had plenty of warning. There had been a rash of bombings, thefts of weapons and arrogant demands by members of the underground group and its supporters. Curiously, many of those involved with the FLQ who instigated the violence—including at least one murder—were strangely remote from events in Canada. One was a Belgian called Schoeters, who like Lee Harvey Oswald had spent eight months in the Soviet Union learning revolutionary tactics; another was François Schrim, an Algerian who led raids on armouries in order to obtain weapons for gangs of militant separatists; some others were of French origin.

There can be no question in the mind of anyone then living in the province, that a determined effort was being made to de-stabilize Quebec society. John Diefenbaker showed me a revolutionary Spanish-language pamphlet printed in Cuba, with diagrams illustrating how to put together an alarm clock bomb. This had been picked up in one of the separatist hideouts.

At the time of the October Crisis, I was writing speeches for Allan MacEachen, then Minister of Manpower and Immigration. Shirley and I had a rather tense dinner with MacEachen at his apartment in Sandy Hill, a quiet, residential neighbourhood in Ottawa, with two heavily armed combat troops sitting in the kitchen. A week later, we underwent the same surreal experience with the Chief and Olive.

I was affected even more strongly by these events because I regarded Pierre Laporte as a friend and colleague. Prior to entering politics, he had been a member of the Press Gallery as a reporter for *Le Devoir*, the Quebec nationalist newspaper. When he came to Aylmer during a provincial election, I took my daughter, Tina, to hear him speak. Later, we chatted with the friendly and charming man. The thought that such an individual should be foully murdered simply for carrying out his duty filled me with revulsion.

A few years later, when I heard René Levesque at the National Press Club accuse Pierre Trudeau of "making political capital of the death of Pierre Laporte," I had the same ugly feeling. With a brief, curt expletive in Levesque's direction, I got up and walked out while the tiny separatist leader screamed denials at me.

The *Globe and Mail* reported that Levesque had been subjected to an "uncouth" interruption. I feel no inclination to apologize.

As Minister of Justice, John Turner had the job of organizing the arrests of those suspected of FLQ connections. Documents recently released reveal that Trudeau wanted the net cast far and wide, with the object of crippling the movement's capacity to act. The documents also reveal that Turner attempted to put the brakes on this course of action, and was bluntly overruled.

Two British journalists, experts on the psychology of terror, provide the best analysis of Trudeau's handling of the October Crisis. In *The Carlos Complex*, *A Study in Terror*, Christopher Dobson of the London *Sunday Express* and Ronald Payne of the *Evening Standard* wrote:

> There is a happier example from Canada where Premier (sic) Trudeau invoked the *War Measures Act* in 1970 and moved in the Army to deal with the Quebec separatists who had kidnapped James Cross, the British Trade Commissioner in Montreal, and Pierre Laporte, Quebec's Minister of Labour and Immigration. When he was criticized for this move, he replied: "There are a lot of bleeding hearts around . . . All I can say is, let them bleed." The FLQ killed Laporte, but Cross was released and although the kidnappers bargained their way to safety on a flight to Cuba, Trudeau's firmness stopped the FLQ's terror campaign and the freedoms that were temporarily sacrificed were later restored in full.

Trudeau, from the viewpoint of Canada's security, acted properly.

Nobody in a free country has a right to support by word or deed an organization responsible for a reign of terror, including murder, kidnapping, theft and violence.

Trudeau believed the primary responsibility of all Canadians, regardless of language or point of origin, was to preserve the unity of the country. He was dead against shutting up in a single province a dynamic race, which had grown from forty thousand in 1759 to nearly six million two centuries later. Quebec controlled education, language, transport, highways, justice, mining, commerce, wildlife, civil law, the courts—in fact, the entire gamut of transactions within its borders. It had a voice in immigration and external relations. It lacked only its own armed forces.

Quebec, as a full partner in Canadian confederation, possessed, in a practical sense, powers and privileges many European countries might envy.

In the 1980s, Pierre Elliott Trudeau brought the constitution "back" to Canada by having it rescinded in Westminster and then passed through the Canadian parliament, unchanged. No one mentioned it had already gone through the Parliament of the United Canadas in 1865 and that the *British North America Act* passed at Westminster in 1867 was almost entirely based on the Quebec Resolutions drawn up and approved in this country by a double majority.

To his "repatriated" constitution, Trudeau attached a Charter of Rights, one feature of which guarantees minority language rights in every province. In every province but Quebec, minority language meant protection for the French language. Then, Trudeau accepted the "notwithstanding" clause proposed by Jean Chrétien and Roy Romanow, which meant, in effect, that any province that didn't want to be bound by the Charter could simply opt out. As for the Charter itself, it simply followed and expanded on Diefenbaker's Bill of Rights of 1961. It was a major public relations ploy. Virtually all of the rights recognized are already guaranteed in English Common Law.

In fact, the Chief refrained from making the Bill of Rights a constitutional amendment because he felt that it was a mistake to "tinker" with the constitution. Trudeau proved him right.

The stand taken by René Levesque, leader of the Parti Québecois and Premier of Quebec, in turning down the Trudeau Constitution in 1982 was taken coldly and deliberately, and after much party discussion. His *separatiste* successors now use it as an argument to say that Quebec was excluded from the Constitution. It was. It excluded itself.

This is not to say the exercise didn't have its merits. It served to remind Canadians they had certain rights and were entitled to have these rights protected by the state. The illusion quickly evaporated when Quebec seized on the notwithstanding clause to ban the English language—spoken by seventy-five per cent of the Canadian population—from public display.

Perhaps Trudeau had a point when he came out against the Charlottetown Accord a few years later with the comment that Quebec had been blackmailing English Canada for years and English-speaking Canadians were stupid enough to let them do it.

He also came out against the earlier Meech Lake Accord—Brian Mulroney's first attempt to bring Quebec "back" into Confederation—on the ground that it granted special recognition to

Quebec. This was the signal for the Liberal Old Guard to stop the Accord at any cost. For Pierre Trudeau, the constitution was a document to be treated like any document. For Sir John A. Macdonald—and John Diefenbaker—the constitution was, quite literally, the backbone of the nation, a vertebra activating the administrative powers of the country. Everything on one side of the line belonged to the federal government, everything on the other side of the line belonged to the provinces. Anyone familiar with the BNA Act knows that Quebec under Meech Lake and, again, in the Charlottetown Accord, got very little more than had already been spelled out in 1867: protection of language, education, Quebec laws as outlined in the Civil Code, a voice in immigration, resource development, and so on.

If these "concessions" constituted dismantling Canada, then it was dismantled in 1867.

Trudeau could rise to great occasions. At other times, he preferred to play possum. There was something Chaplinesque about his rapidly changing roles. He could lead a mad parade of journalists across Parliament Hill, slide down banisters and dive, swanlike, from springboards. He could also rise up in the House and, in a dull monotonous voice with a look of complete innocence, announce a national energy policy whereby the federal government would tax away profits of western oil companies at a time when OPEC had hoisted prices sky high.

What Trudeau was actually proposing was that the government should run the petroleum industry from the East Block, a ploy with obvious shortcomings.

One thing wrong with the plan, which involved special taxes and so-called exploration incentives, was that the bureaucrats assumed oil prices would remain out of sight for the foreseeable future. OPEC made the same assumption. However, a few months after the introduction of the National Energy Policy, the United States responded to the oil crisis by cutting back its consumption by twenty-five per cent. The Middle Eastern oil barons had oil coming out their ears. But the damage was already done. An exodus of Canadian oil producers streamed to the United States leaving the Trudeau government with a costly, cumbersome and irrelevant piece of bureaucratic machinery, which seemed to have no purpose other than to drain capital from the West to fat cat Central Canada.

In the 1979 election, this was one of the factors that brought victory to Joe Clark's Tories.

It was then that Pierre Trudeau decided to take a walk in the snow and leave politics aside for the time being. This opened the door for the improbable candidacy of Joe Clark.

CHAPTER 19

John Turner to the Rescue

IT WAS JOHN TURNER all the way at the 1984 Liberal Party Convention. He beat Jean Chrétien for the leadership, took over from Pierre Trudeau as prime minister, then almost immediately called an election.

Some analysts thought Turner should have hung in, making a stab at running the country for a year or so and calling an election from a position of strength. Turner had received a sort of reluctant laying on of hands from Pierre Trudeau, but he wasn't elected, and he felt the sooner his position could become legitimized by an election, the more comfortable he would feel.

While it does not appear Turner had any doubts about his capacity to win, he could not have been in any doubt about the feelings of the party hierarchy—the Trudeau Old Guard—with regard to himself. They didn't like him and didn't want him.

Grattan O'Leary told me a story that Turner told him. It illustrates the point perfectly.

Following the 1974 election, after deriding Stanfield's statement that he was going to control prices, Trudeau set up a kind of makeshift board to review the price structure in the country. Two Liberal friends of mine, Dick O'Hagan and Jean-Luc Pepin, were in charge. I was seconded to assist. One of the problems was that while the group was active in monitoring prices, it did little or nothing about holding down wages, except for a kind of goody-goody twoshoes slogan, known as "six and five," a cap on public service salaries.

Turner, as Minister of Finance in the Trudeau government, was troubled by the way in which the wages and prices issue was being handled. According to the story he told Grattan, he went in to see Trudeau in order to get support for a tough, hands-on approach. Sensing the prime minister's lack of interest, he decided the situation called for a show of firmness. Bluntly, he told Trudeau that if he didn't get support, he would have to consider resigning. At that, Trudeau came round from behind his desk to grasp Turner's hand.

"I certainly hate to see you go. How would you like the Senate?"

That was the way, according to Turner, that he walked out of the Trudeau government in September 1975.

It was one of the longest pouts in history, lasting until June 1984, when he returned to confront Trudeau as the new Liberal leader. Even then, Trudeau demanded his pound of flesh from Turner, the man he had let go.

According to Turner's version—never contradicted—Trudeau handed him a list covering more than a score of patronage appointments of MPs, former MPs and ministers, and members of Trudeau's office staff and insisted they constitute Turner's first order of business as prime minister. Attempting to explain his action in the television debate with Mulroney, Turner said, "I had no choice."

This brought Mulroney's riposte which, to some, was the deciding moment in the campaign.

"You had a choice, sir. You could have refused."

Senate appointments on Trudeau's last day in office included four former Liberal ministers, the son of a former Liberal minister and two of the prime minister's personal staff. One of Trudeau's last-minute appointments was that of his deputy prime minister, Allan J. MacEachen.

The appointments were ratified by the new prime minister, John Turner.

Turner felt called on in the middle of the campaign to fire Bill Lee, his campaign director, and replace him with Keith Davey, who was closely attached to the Trudeau Old Guard. This turned out to be a major error on John Turner's part.

According to Senator Davey in his book, *The Rainmaker*, one of Turner's major problems in the election was his determination to distance himself from Trudeau, his predecessor.

He may have had his reasons.

Trudeau waited until the election was under way before publicly contradicting Turner's version of why he left the Trudeau government. He didn't call Turner a liar; he simply said the version given by Turner to reporters aboard the campaign aircraft didn't match his own recollection. For a former prime minister to contradict his successor in the middle of an election on a point so abstruse was not calculated to win votes. The statement constituted a stab in the back by Pierre Trudeau.

John Turner's real problem was that he had been away too long. His party connections had withered and atrophied. He got only token support from the party apparatus and none at all from the Trudeau Old Guard.

Turner was like a hockey player trying for a comeback. His slap shot had lost some of its zing, his stick handling wasn't quite as impeccable, and even his skates weren't as sharp.

When the John Turner of 1975 patted a female behind, it was an occasion. When the older, rumpled, white-haired John Turner of 1984 laid a less than respectful palm on the august posterior of Liberal Party president, Iona Campagnola, he was just a dirty old man.

When the election was over, Brian Mulroney was the new Prime Minister of Canada. John Turner was out, after enjoying the fruits of office for exactly ten weeks, making Joe Clark appear a model of longevity.

With victory, the new prime minister, Brian Mulroney, achieved the goal on which his energies had been fixed for most of his adult life. Mulroney pulled off the event in grand style, leading the Tories back to office with the largest majority in history: 211 out of 285 seats.

To reach his goal, he had created an organization, bound friends to his cause, stepped over Joe Clark and knocked out John Turner.

Now, he had arrived.

Now, at last, he would unfold his agenda for Canada.

CHAPTER 20

At Home with Brian Mulroney

AS ANYONE who has had anything to do with him knows, Brian Mulroney has a plentiful supply of Irish charm. It worked with US President Ronald Reagan and his successor, George Bush. Both presidents and their wives admired the Mulroneys and maintained a relationship of friendly, informal intimacy with Brian and Mila. This was one reason why Canada got a free trade deal with the United States that no other country could get.

Another prominent Irish quality of Brian's led him into considerable trouble: the Irishman's inevitable compulsion to surround himself with tried and true friends whose selection was based on the single criterion of loyalty. As often happens, some were loyal only to their own interests.

So who, deep down, is Brian Mulroney?

First, and above all, he is a Quebec Irishman. This meant he has spent most of his life trying to fit in, to be part of a culture essentially foreign to himself. That he has done this so successfully indicates a tremendous capacity for taking on the colour of his surroundings, for presenting one visage to the world around him and maintaining for himself an inner personality seldom revealed.

I felt I understood something about Mulroney because I, too, am of Irish background with a tincture of Dutch on my father's side. On my mother's side, we are Gatineau Irish: the Graces of Gracefield, with some Doyles and Ringroses thrown in for good measure. On both sides, I am fourth-generation Quebecker. As to my family's roots in America, there is a gravestone in Kinderhook, New York, bearing the name Van Dusen and the date, 1628. I have never felt any compulsion to explain my antecedents to people like Jacques Parizeau, who coined the phrase, "vielle souche," to draw a line between original French inhabitants and newcomers. I am willing to match my roots against Mr Parizeau's any time. My *souche* is at least as *vieille*, even though my *laine* may not be as pure.

I felt I knew where Brian Mulroney was coming from and he knew where I was coming from.

He was coming from the same place as Daniel Johnson, Claude Ryan and all those Quebec Irish who, after trying to prove something to the English for three hundred years, were now in Quebec trying to prove the same thing to French Canadians: that they were as good as everyone else. I have never felt any compulsion to make that point. I assumed everyone took it for granted.

When I was active in Quebec politics (I ran twice for parliament in the Gatineau), I used to attend organizational meetings from time to time when Daniel Johnson, then a Quebec minister and a coming force in the Union Nationale, gathered with a dozen or so stalwarts in a hotel room in Hull, across the river from Ottawa.

As everyone was leaving, Johnson would say in French, "Hold on, Van. I'd like to talk to you."

As soon as the last organizer was out of the room, Johnson would switch to English.

"All right, Van. Let's talk."

When Daniel Johnson's father arrived from Ireland, he couldn't speak a word of French. Dan did a lot better, becoming premier in the process, as have both his sons—Daniel and Pierre-Marc—who are also accepted as fully French-Canadian.

The road of assimilation, so deplored by language nationalists, runs in both directions.

Mulroney represented a new equation in Canadian politics: a perfectly bilingual English-Canadian. Had he succeeded in including the Meech Lake Accord in the Constitution, the Tories would have held Quebec for a generation. This simple fact accounts for the frantic opposition drummed up by the Liberal Party, beginning with Trudeau's personal attack on Mulroney, followed by Clyde Wells' reneging on Newfoundland's approval and Sharon Carstairs' last ditch attempt to forestall approval in the Manitoba legislature.

Mulroney had a lot going for him. In his mid-forties with a mastery of both languages, an impeccable Quebec background, and an attractive family, he was tailor-made to fill the Conservative Party's need for a Quebec leader. It was like getting a younger, French-speaking version of John Diefenbaker. Brian was, almost literally, a text book candidate.

Mila, his beautiful and charming wife, had a background in the Slavic community and was mother to their three attractive children. Brian was as close as you could come to an English-language equivalent of Pierre Trudeau, without the slight handicap of inherited wealth. Mulroney's father was a blue-collar electrician in the Baie Comeau paper mill. Brian came up the hard way; working his way through university and, later, law school at Laval. At St Francis Xavier University in Nova Scotia, Allan MacEachen was one of his professors.

While studying at Laval, Brian used to come up to the House to see the Chief. At the same time, Joe Clark was working at headquarters as head of the party's youth wing. By the time the 1965 election rolled around, both, with the impatience of youth, had come to believe the Chief had outlived his time. Eventually, both had to confront the harsh realities of leading the party and the country.

For the non-French-Canadian in Quebec, there is a constant need to assert your identity and individuality. You are always aware that no matter how well you may have mastered the language and even the thinking of the French-Canadian collectivity, you remain outside the stockade. This is not to say that French-Canadians are not receptive, sympathetic and welcoming to those who meet them half way. They are. As far as I'm concerned, they're my brothers. I know Mulroney felt the same.

Moving in the English-Canadian milieu, the Quebec Irishman, or, for that matter, any Irishman, still feels the necessity to impress on others the fact of his existence. In a milieu that is more restrained, more cautious and less out-going, this approach sometimes appears exaggerated and forward.

Mulroney knew something about politics, but he had a lot to learn about parliament. He soon learned what others had learned: the House is the most important platform in the country. And, with the cameras recording the action, the impact of parliament is magnified.

Repeatedly, I had to emphasize that the people across the aisle were not his friends; nor were they influenced by Irish charm. Purely and simply put, they were out to get him, to make him look fatuous. We managed to meet the test of the first few months. Mulroney was a "quick study" in theatrical terms. It didn't take long for him to get the mood and swing of the House, to realize it was much like hockey, a game he'd been good at. The trick was to keep hold of the puck. The same applied in the House; the puck being the issue at stake.

As Joe Clark learned, there is no on-the-job training for prime ministers. You either know what you're doing, or you're out in the next election. People don't make allowances for amateurs. They watch and judge. And that's the way it should be.

Mulroney had handled a large corporation and had been active in Quebec public life. The House was different, as Tommy Douglas and George Drew found out. It is the most inhospitable, most callous, most unforgiving and most merciless audience in the world.

As T.C. Douglas rose to make his maiden appeal to parliament, someone yelled out, "Get up off your knees."

In the face of the bellicose and sometimes bombastic George Drew, the House yawned its boredom.

A prime minister must master the House, so that when he or she stands, silence falls. Diefenbaker always had the gift, while Pearson always looked like somebody addressing a public service symposium. Mulroney did manage to come to terms with the chamber; not in the way of Diefenbaker or Paul Martin Sr, but at least as well as Mike Pearson or George Drew.

Mulroney brought to Parliament Hill a Quebec political persona that sometimes rasped. Trudeau, although a product of the same province, managed to leave behind, to all appearances, those peculiarly Quebec observances that grate on English Canada. Trudeau was not above using offensive, sometimes obscene language and gestures in public; but, somehow, it was always apparent that he was playing a game.

Brian Mulroney, in typical Quebec style, surrounded himself with close friends, many of them sycophants and flatterers, others whose past performances did not bear scrutiny. Consulting firms sprang up, made up of people close to the prime minister. And, after the 1984 election, I found myself immediately in the middle of a struggle over offices.

The principle was a simple one.

The closer the office to the prime minister, the greater the status of the incumbent. Personally, all I wanted was a place to work.

Pat MacAdam had occupied the adjoining office to the leader on the fourth floor while in opposition. When we moved down to the prime minister's suite, I was told I would have that honour. It turned out to be the same office I used when working for the Chief. I felt it belonged to Pat, who had worked for Brian Mulroney for several years, had publicly supported him and was a personal friend. I had no desire to be caught in a squeeze play over offices.

I went down to see Pat in his new office overlooking the front lobby of the Centre Block, to the left of the Peace Tower. It had two rooms and had belonged to a Liberal minister. However, so that there would be no mistake, Pat had a brass plate on the door saying "PRIME MINISTER'S OFFICE." This turned out to be inconvenient, as tourists kept barging in expecting to see Brian Mulroney.

I made it clear to Pat I didn't want the office beside the PM. I offered to switch, but he declined. I learned during the Diefenbaker days if you got too close to the stove, you got burned when the heat went up. Plus, when I wanted to leave early, I had to walk in front of the prime minister's door. I felt embarrassed by his accusing look. Fred Doucette, Mulroney's Chief of Staff, came to me a few weeks later to say the pressure of work demanded he take the office next to the PM and would I mind moving? I was happy to oblige in a game of musical chairs or musical offices. By this time, I was beginning to wonder whether I was in a school for backward students.

Unrelenting as some sections of the media were in finding fault with Mulroney—from the shoes on his feet (or in his closet), to his wife's preferences in home furnishings, to his government's policies—not all of his image problems were media induced. Many were, in fact, the obverse of strategies adopted to deal with specific problems.

One of the curious facts, however, which will strike the objective witness, is that all of the major Mulroney government policies—the Canada-US Trade Deal, the GST, full participation in peace-keeping—were still in effect after the Liberals secured their second mandate in 1997.

Every Conservative leader since Macdonald has suffered from Quebec's tendency to vote as a block for the Liberal Party. To break the Liberal stranglehold, Mulroney had to go even farther than the Liberals in winning Quebec support. The Manitoba language issue and the transfer of the CF-18 maintenance contract to Canadair in Montreal from Bristol Aerospace in Winnipeg are prime examples. However, each step that Mulroney took in persuading Quebec voters of his attachment to their interests antagonized an equal number of voters in Western Canada. Thus, he was caught in the classic dilemma of Tory leaders.

Gordon Churchill's advice to Diefenbaker—ignore Quebec and pile up votes in the rest of the country—proved unworkable.

According to John Laschinger and Geoffrey Stevens, in their book, *Leaders and Lesser Mortals*, the Grits had polls done showing that if there was a weakness in the public perception of Mulroney, it was the area of trust. So, Grit strategists and spin doctors immediately zeroed in on that issue. Could Mulroney be trusted? Obviously not. If he held a meeting with premiers, as spelled out in the constitution, it was a session "behind closed doors" out of which must come a "secret deal." The press printed all this claptrap as if it was Gospel.

This was a tactic very familiar to me from Diefenbaker days. In Quebec, the Grits said the Chief would remove the habits from the nuns. In fact, it wasn't John Diefenbaker who accomplished that. It was the Pope.

Mulroney also had serious problems with his Quebec MPs. Since there was no provincial Conservative Party, his followers, perforce, came from the nationalist or separatist ranks, constituting a source of permanent embarrassment. A feeling grew that Mulroney was prepared to favour Quebec's interests over those of Canada for political reasons.

This charge had also been levelled against the Pearson government, but that was a Liberal government and Liberal governments are expected to play up to Quebec. And that was before a Quebec government, complaining with one side of its mouth about being put down by English-speaking Canada, had taken steps to ban public display of the English language—the first time in recorded history that an oppressed society has banned the language of the oppressor. This, more than any other action or claim by Quebec, antagonized English-speaking Canadians from coast to coast, to whom it appeared that the oppression was on the other foot; and the foot was, quite literally, in Quebec's mouth.

To this ill-advised action can be traced much of the opposition to the Meech Lake and Charlottetown Accords. However, Mulroney, like many raised in Quebec and conditioned to the endless assertion of Quebec particularity—an inherited obsession—did not immediately recognize the deep, astringent bitterness of English-speaking Canadians. It became unmistakably apparent in time, as a man named Clyde Wells picked up the ball and ran with it.

When Brian Mulroney swept into power in 1984 with the largest majority in Canadian history—211 out of a possible 285 seats—he had been a member of parliament for thirteen months. Technically that made him a novice. Most of his advisors knew virtually nothing about the workings of either government or the parliamentary system. Compare this to the fact that Lester Pearson served as an MP for fifteen years before becoming leader, while John Diefenbaker sat in the House for seventeen years before reaching the highest goal in Canadian politics.

Mulroney's lack of experience meant he could not judge the effect of an action or motion in the House. Secondly, he had no background with which to measure the reaction in the House as compared to the reaction in the country. However, he overcame these serious disabilities by his second term. It also didn't take him long to realize Ottawa played by a different set of rules.

In provincial politics, personal vindication and patronage are acceptable, but not in Ottawa. A federal government has to view issues in broad, general terms, from the viewpoint of the nation's welfare.

Those who accused Mulroney of having no clear vision of Canada as expressed in policy statements failed to take the man's measure. His policies came out of two sets of experiences: First, his familiarity with Canada-US trading practices and his knowledge of international trade born from many trips to Europe and Asia; and, second, his day-to-day understanding of political ideas and thought currents in the province of Quebec.

His business and commercial background was second to that of no other modern prime minister and rivalled only by that of C.D. Howe, Minister of Trade under Mackenzie King. His knowledge of Quebec's organic make-up was visceral, matched only by Trudeau and, in some ways, more basic.

His business background meant he favoured a policy of breaking Canada out of the cocoon of economic dependence on the United States. This became increasingly urgent in view of Europe's steps towards economic union. His trade policy thus stood on increased exports to the US, but also on the consequences of Canadian isolation.

Overriding all other concerns was the pressing issue of the huge debt run up under the Trudeau administration, which was costing the government twenty-four cents on every dollar when Mulroney came to power; and, an additional ten cents by the middle of his second term. The government was, therefore, being taxed at an ever-increasing rate by its own debt load.

All of the policy permutations of the Mulroney government revolved round these salient points: to bring Canada into the mainstream of international trading relationships on the basis of competitive skill, so that Canadian workmanship could compete fairly in the world market. This could not happen if the country wrapped itself up in a trade blanket with restrictive federal policies substituting for free market competition. This was clearly demonstrated in the botched federal petroleum policy.

Secondly, Quebec must play a vital and dynamic constitutional role as a full and willing partner, rather than being dragged along for the ride. This meant a willingness to listen and meet Quebec's anxieties with positive measures in the interest of preserving the national fabric.

The attempts to reach a constitutional accord in the Meech Lake and Charlottetown Agreements related to Mulroney's perceived need to deal with the Quebec issue and to pull the rug out from under those who wished to dismantle the country.

Mulroney represented a new power equation in Canadian politics. Since Laurier, the Liberals had held power with Quebec support. Mulroney robbed them of their Quebec fiefdom. The Tories, solid in the West and Ontario, standing for the old British virtues of Flag and Empire—now both gone—had to carve out a new venue. With Mulroney they did so; the new venue was Quebec.

The Liberals couldn't afford for the Tories to secure Quebec, which is why Chrétien, Trudeau and Lalonde fought the Meech Lake Accord with all the resources at their command. When Mulroney went back to the bargaining table with the ill-fated Charlottetown

Accord (Meech Lake reborn), it was the separatists themselves who fought tooth and nail against it. Not to have done so would have removed a major grievance from the separatist litany of charges against the federal government.

Mulroney's fiscal policies, Free Trade, and the GST were put in place and remain. His constitutional moves, aimed at bringing Quebec back in the fold after the 1982 walkout, were doomed to failure because too many divergent political forces had an interest in seeing them fail.

CHAPTER 21

Trouble in Paradise

THE GRITS were in power, Brian Mulroney was leader of the Tory Party, winter was coming on, so it seemed like a good time to go on a cruise.

In February 1983, Shirley and I flew to the Dominican Republic where we boarded *Azur*, a 15,000-ton French liner with a crew of 250 dedicated to satisfying the whims and desires of the 700 passengers. As we sailed down the Caribbean Archipelago to Barbados, the only thing to disturb our tranquil surroundings was the news of trouble in Grenada. The prime minister, Maurice Bishop, a Castro protégé, was under house arrest, his government taken over by a Soviet-sponsored junta. I had asked Brian Mulroney for a letter to signify that I had "his confidence." I knew Barbados was very concerned about the growing Soviet and Cuban intervention.

Azur was out of *Joseph Conrad* by Somerset Maugham: rattan tables and chairs in the afterdeck bar, a majestic pool and palatial saloon, a finely appointed cocktail bar amidships, and tiny boutiques to add a touch of class. As we ploughed through the Caribbean nights, an orchestra provided music you could actually dance to. I was standing in front of the saloon bar in white jacket and pants, wearing my yachting cap with the words "Fisherman's Wharf" stencilled on it, when a woman came out of the bar.

"Are you official?"

I drew myself up.

"Very official, madam."

"Can you take me to my cabin?"

"Certainly, madam."

She gave me a suspicious look.

"You're not official."

"Whatever you say, madam."

She went back in the bar and I went on deck where I leaned on the rail and watched the moon splash the Caribbean with gold.

We passed a dark, looming shape with a cluster of lights. The island of Montserrat, the chart in the saloon told me. This rang a bell. I remembered receiving letters from an uncle, Father Tom Grace, while I was still at university. He talked about Montserrat and the chapel he was building for people who had to walk nine miles to mass. Every night he went to bed with bleeding hands from working with coral rock.

An RCAF chaplain, Father Tom had been severely reprimanded during the war for accompanying flight crews on bombing missions over Germany. His excuse was that, in order to understand the crews' problems, he had to know what they went through.

Tom Van Dusen hard at work on his favourite island, Barbados.

After the war, he was handed a rich and comfortable living in Bermuda. This would have been enough for most clergy, but Father Tom asked for a transfer to the islands, where he could work with poor black people, rather than rich whites. He found himself on Montserrat.

A year after our cruise, our daughter Tina and her husband, Stuart, went to Montserrat and found Father Tom's chapel, a beautiful building of cut coral. Even though Father Tom was dead, his memory was revered. Today, after the recent volcano that blanketed the island, the chapel is buried in ash.

Shirley and I arrived in Barbados to learn that a Soviet-sponsored group had ruthlessly shot down Prime Minister Bishop in Grenada. Afterwards, I went to the Government Building, formerly the Marine Hotel, and found the Foreign Secretary, Brazane Babb, behind a mountain of papers. I showed him Brian Mulroney's letter and said, "I want you to know that the Conservative Party of Canada is very much behind the position taken by the Commonwealth Caribbean countries."

Brazane Babb expressed his appreciation on behalf of the prime minister, Tom Adams, who was a major mover—along with Eugenia Charles, Prime Minister of Dominica, Edward Compton, Prime Minister of Antigua and Edward Seaga, Prime Minister of Jamaica, in Caribbean affairs. Prime Minister Adams had been following the proceedings in Canada's parliament.

The Caribbean was the "back yard" of the United States. For Canada, the Caribbean, where we have been carrying on trade for three hundred years, is our front yard.

Barbados, Jamaica, Antigua and several others eventually requested American intervention to restore order and free the people of Grenada from the rule of the Soviet-sponsored junta, which soon assumed complete power, including the small Grenada Army. In view of the overt participation of Cuba and the Soviet Union in the outbreak of brutal violence on Grenada, they felt the same fate might be waiting for them.

President Ronald Reagan, holidaying in Augusta, Georgia, was awakened early in the morning of October 22, 1983, by a call from Secretary of State George Schultz. He informed the president that a number of Caribbean countries headed by Barbados and Jamaica were asking for US military intervention to head off a fullscale communist takeover of Grenada and restore order amid conditions of anarchy and chaos. After consulting Vice President George Bush, who had chaired a Caribbean security meeting the day before in Washington, Reagan decided to move in. A force of US Marines on its way to the Middle East received orders to divert to the Caribbean. Twelve warships were soon on their way, led by the carrier *Independence*. The force included five hundred marines and one thousand rangers from the First and Second Battalions of the 75th.

Almost as though deliberately intended to distract the US mission, a car-bomb attack in Beirut brought death to more than two hundred marines in the Middle East. Reagan refused to be diverted and on October 25, 1983, the Americans moved.

When the marines landed, weapons had already been made available to the seven hundred Cuban "airport workers" on the island, who were, coincidentally, nearly all members of Castro's militia under the command of Colonel Tomas y Tortola. He had arrived in Grenada after the assassination of Maurice Bishop. The Canadian government seemed to have been left in the dark. One reason, perhaps, might have been the statement by Eugenia Charles. She said the Caribbean Commonwealth Federation—CARICOM—didn't trust the Trudeau government.

The Soviets had built up a military arsenal on Grenada following an agreement signed in Moscow with the Grenada government on July 27, 1982, whereby the Soviets agreed to deliver weaponry valued at ten million rubles to the island by 1985. Prime Minister Bishop had gone to Moscow to plead with the Russians for a commercial airport that would bring tourists to Grenada from all over the world. The Russians insisted on a military airport that would enable them to deliver military supplies to guerrilla groups in El Salvador and Nicaragua. Shortly afterwards, Bishop was placed under house arrest.

I have a copy of the arms agreement. It is signed by Lieutenant Colonel Liam James, a dedicated Marxist, on behalf of the Government of Grenada, and an indecipherable Russian name, on behalf of the Soviet Union. A friend who worked on the airport told me it was quite obviously designed to deal with Soviet military transports.

The military hardware forwarded in Soviet ships to the tiny Caribbean island included, according to the agreement in Russian and

English, armoured personnel carriers, 100,000 cartridges, 30 76 mm ZIZ3 guns with 1,000 armourpiercing shells, anti-tank weapons and portable rocket launchers with 1,800 rockets. It also included 60 82mm mortars with 21,600 fragmentation mines to be fired from those same mortars, 50 antitank grenade launchers, 60 PKM machine-guns; 30 PKMS machine-guns, 270 62mm DPM machine-guns with 919,000 cartridges, 2,000 sub-machine-guns, 1,000 carbines, 10 snipers' rifles (favoured for assassinations), 150 9mm pistols, more than 5,000 mines, various items of communications equipment, and even 1,500 pairs of black cotton socks. Enough to equip a brigade. And, by this time, much of the weaponry had already been delivered and was being stored in warehouses at the Port Salines Airport.

One is led irresistibly to the conclusion that the Soviets were equipping a major force on Grenada to be used in further military adventures. And, more than anything else, it was this attempt to extend Soviet power in Central and South America that concerned the US. It should, of course, have been of major concern to Canada.

The Cuban "workers," under the command of Colonel Tortola, succeeded in bringing down a Sea King helicopter with a Soviet missile.

When the Americans arrived, Sea King helicopters swung in over the island, Rangers armed to the teeth floated down like exotic birds in the pink light of dawn, and 130 gunships laid down a bristling carpet of 6,000 rounds per minute. It was a carpet on which no one could walk and live. It was only a matter of days before Grenada was under control and the governor general, Sir Paul Scoons, was in charge.

Sixteen months after the invasion he had helped to launch, Prime Minister Tom Adams of Barbados was found dead, sprawled on a divan in the prime minister's residence. Cause of death was attributed to a heart attack. A few months earlier, I saw the prime minister dash up the steps of the Government Building to his second-floor office, looking very much unlike a man with a heart problem. Barbados, by the way, had contributed a force of some four hundred soldiers to help maintain order in Grenada.

A few months later, Shirley and I visited the prime minister's residence during a reception and I viewed the room where Tom

Adams had been found. It is a big room with windows opening onto a garden. Music from the Barbados Police Band came wafting in on the gentle Caribbean breeze. Crowds roamed the grounds amongst tables temptingly spread with food and drink set up under the trees. It was a beautiful setting, but this palatial home of a former British governor had remained unused as a residence since Adams' death, his successor, Errol Barrow, declining to live there.

CHAPTER 22

The Face of Scandal

SCANDALS ERUPTED around the Mulroney government like mushrooms after rain.

This was not totally unexpected, since in Ottawa, uncovering scandals is a cottage industry, second only to creating them.

Opposition members survey those in power with all the scrutiny of espionage agents in a James Bond movie.

In politics, scandal is a paying proposition. It destroys governments and helps opposition attain power.

Scandal pays in the media. It creates TV viewers, boosts ratings and sells newspapers.

The great national parties—the Grits and Tories—are not above playing spy games on one another. The Liberals, for example, had a "mole" in Conservative headquarters for a number of years. More power to him. I hope he was able to find out more than the party members ever did.

When I moved into the Tory Party, I discovered someone was investigating the private lives of Grits. I stopped it. It wasn't my cup of tea, or John Diefenbaker's either.

As allegations piled up surrounding the activities of the Mulroney government, however, it appeared some of the friends and supporters of the government were not only greedy, but stupid. When government contracts were involved, friendly lobbyists turned up in negotiations as advisers and consultants; not unheard of in the practices of governments, yet it is hard to discern what services these political insiders could contribute to the appraisal of military helicopters, electric components of army tanks or airport design. That's probably better left to the imagination.

My activities at this time were largely restricted to preparing the prime minister for the House; and yet, one would have had to be on another planet to be unaware of the swirling currents of self-help and the strong suggestion that pounds of flesh were being demanded for services sometimes of a doubtful nature.

Incidentally, all political scandals are "affairs," not mere happenings.

In the Oerlikon Affair, the campaign manager for André Bissonette, Minister of Small Business, declined to turn over $1 million placed in a trust fund in his name by Oerlikon, a Swiss company that had received a multi-million dollar contract for military electronics. André Bissonette was a millionaire who ran a string of chicken outlets and this contract had been awarded in his riding of St-Jean. Although cleared in court of having any personal interest in the transaction, he did not run again and vanished from the political scene.

Oerlikon's lawyer in the episode, Jean Bazin, was named to the Senate by Mulroney. They had been friends for many years. After Bissonette was cleared, Bazin, on behalf of Oerlikon, demanded the million dollars be returned. Bazin has since resigned from the Senate.

This affair left its mark, as did the activities of Senator Michel Cogger, a friend of the prime minister's for many years, who was involved in a court action brought by a Japanese investor against a Quebec businessman. Charged with influence peddling, Cogger claimed he had been paid for legal advice and counsel. There was no evidence that he had been instrumental in securing contracts from the Mulroney Government.

Roch Lasalle, a minister Mulroney inherited from Joe Clark, was accused of accepting money from contractors. Insufficient evidence came forth to provide a basis for charges in a court of law.

The so-called "Tainted Tuna" Affair cast a shadow over the government and brought on the resignation of the minister responsible, John Fraser.

Fisheries Department inspectors removed from store shelves a brand of tuna which they ruled unfit for human consumption. The minister, apparently bowing to pressure, ordered the ban rescinded. This caused an uproar in the media and the House. Damage control became the order of the day.

I confess I was not, perhaps, as helpful as I might have been.

I first heard of the affair when a reporter phoned me one night in the prime minister's office to ask when I first became aware of the tainted tuna scandal. This was one of those loaded questions along the lines of "When did you stop beating your wife?" If you answered that you knew all along, then you were a part of the cover-up. If you said you knew nothing about it, no matter what it was, then you looked stupid. I decided to tell the truth and look stupid.

I said, "Just now."

"You mean to say you knew nothing about the tainted tuna before?"

"I still don't know anything about it. What is it? I don't like tuna."

I suggested it would be a good idea to ask the minister responsible, but the media obviously wanted to involve the prime minister.

Next morning, there was a high-level damage control meeting in the prime minister's office in the Centre Block, including top ministers, functionaries and advisors, as well as the Minister of Fisheries, John Fraser. Mulroney went around the room, asking each one what should be done. My answer was simple and straightforward. The minister should stand up in his place in the House, present a tin of tuna and a can opener, open the tuna, take out a fork and eat it with every sign of enjoyment. With the cameras focused on the minister, the dramatic scene would go round the country.

"He should smack his lips and eat right to the bottom of the tin. You'll never hear any more about it."

For my pains, I received a long, cool stare from the prime minister and smothered guffaws from the others. Without comment, Mulroney went on to the next person. I believe it was the Finance Minister, Michael Wilson, who could obviously see nothing humorous in the suggestion. In the end, John Fraser resigned.

Later, in the lobby, I said to Pat Nowlan, in whose Nova Scotia riding the cannery was located, "Why didn't Fraser do what I suggested? The media would have bought it, hook, line and sinker."

Roaring with laughter, Nowlan replied, "He probably would have thrown up."

I still think it was a good idea. It would have ended the controversy then and there. Instead, it dragged on for the better part of a week. To coin a phrase, the tainted tuna remained an albatross round the neck of the Mulroney government.

John Fraser was redeemed when, with majority support from the members, he went on to become one of the great Speakers of Parliament.

One day, I got a call from a friend in the Press Gallery warning me of a scandal about to break, involving the Minister of National Defence, Bob Coates, for whom I always had great personal respect. In fact, I had campaigned with him in his Nova Scotia riding during the 1958 election.

Erik Nielsen was now in charge of ethics and assured me that everything was under control. That day, the story broke in the *Ottawa Citizen*. It turned out that Coates, while on tour in West Germany, had had a drink with a show girl named Mickey O'Neill in a night club in Lahr.

With a name like Mickey O'Neill, they were probably discussing the troubles in Ireland.

National Defence bigwigs were scandalized at the idea of a minister having drinks with a show girl. A few years later, they had bigger worries in Somalia.

Mulroney was out of the country. Erik got in touch and persuaded the PM that the only solution was Bob Coates' resignation. That afternoon, under pressure from Erik Nielsen, a crest-fallen Bob Coates stood up before a full House and stepped down as minister. The episode, it seemed to me, made Canada a laughing stock of the world.

I had the feeling parliamentarians were allowing themselves to be treated like school boys. If every politician who had a drink in a bar with a show girl resigned, who'd be left? We were imposing standards on elected representatives that no one would think of imposing on themselves. Applying the same standards to the media, there'd be a spate of vacancies in the Parliamentary Press Gallery.

The media sitting in judgement can only be justified on the issue of a member or minister's capacity to carry out his sworn duties. However, what started out in print journalism as a reasonable application of criteria by reasonable people, in the intense competition generated by television, had become a kind of watching and besetting by the media hoping to trap a public figure for the sake of a headline or news clip. Yellow journalism was making a comeback as television news competed with entertainment for the fragmented audience and print tried desperately to keep up.

Not only must there be no evil, there must be no appearance of evil. That was all very well for Caesar's wife, but a member of parliament is not Caesar's wife. Government is not a Sunday school. When it becomes one, it will forfeit its capacity to act broadly, generously and with openness. This is not a defence of weakness or turpitude, but a plea for a sense of proportion.

A government leader is not a house detective. A prime minister, or premier, for that matter, cannot know at every hour of the day and night what the members of his or her government and caucus are up to. Nor, despite what some may think, has a leader control over his or her members. They are adults, people of experience, responsible men and women with a right to live their own private and personal lives. Ministers, however, are in a different situation.

There are stories of the Chief calling members and even ministers in and dressing them down on the subject of their sexual activities. It did not noticeably produce a deterring effect.

As a means of showing concern and appropriate action, governments have favoured codes of conduct or ethics, which have had approximately the same effect as the Ten Commandments and the Laws of Hammurabi. When people are honest and straightforward, codes of ethics are unnecessary. When they are not, codes of ethics are irrelevant.

There were other embarrassments still to come.

Sinc Stevens first came into my ken back in the early sixties when, as chairman of British International Finance, he allowed himself to be drawn into the orbit of the group attempting to remove John Diefenbaker from the leadership. When the Chief began asking questions in the House, BIF's stock slipped. Later, Sinc joined James E. Coyne, former Governor of the Bank of Canada, in a venture to establish a Bank of Western Canada. This went by the boards.

It will be remembered that in the 1976 Leadership Convention, it was Sinc Steven's public support for Joe Clark that got him the leadership. Joe thanked Sinc three years later by appointing him President of the Privy Council, where he performed with competence and panache. Mulroney, in turn, inherited Sinc when he came to power in 1984.

Inside the Tent

In 1983, I worked closely with Sinc during the Grenada Affair. When it came out that the Americans didn't trust the Trudeau government to keep quiet about their proposed intervention in Grenada—a distrust shared by several CARICOM countries—the Trudeau government was in an embarrassing position. Sinc capitalized on this situation by lobbing searching questions in the House, fuelled with information I was able to provide him from my contacts in the Caribbean.

When the *Globe and Mail* revealed that a loan of $2.6 million had been made to Sinc's wife by a former executive of Magna International, Anton Zapka, Sinc found himself in hot water, even though he had fulfilled the requirements of the government's ethics code by removing himself from his business interests, which were being administered by his wife.

The prime minister was in Japan when the story broke, leaving Erik Nielsen to handle the issue, day after day, in the House. At the end of his second week on the griddle, Erik told me that he was quitting.

"My credibility is gone."

"I don't believe that."

"You're a minority of one."

He had already forwarded his resignation to the prime minister.

About this time, Mulroney called me at home one night.

"I want your advice about what I should do about these scandals."

"You've got to get rid of some of the people who are dragging down the government, Prime Minister."

"Some of these people are my friends."

"A prime minister has no friends."

"Maybe you're right."

Within weeks, the house cleaning began. People began leaving the Mulroney entourage, the PMO and the House staff. New faces appeared, including Derek Burney, a career public servant of unimpeachable integrity, to restore the credibility of the office. Burney went to work with a will. Later, he performed in outstanding fashion as Canada's ambassador in Washington.

The fact that scandal plagued the new Mulroney government should not surprise anyone. Every government at every level has its share of such affairs and the number of convictions in the Mulroney government compares with most proceeding governments, including both Pearson's and Trudeau's. In fact, the story of corruption is as old as the country. The affinity between people who have large sums of public money at their disposal and other people who would like to separate them from it, at times, seems almost preordained.

The Fantasy Gardens fiasco forced out BC's Premier Bill Vander Zalm, some of whose fantasies turned out to be all too real in a political context. In Ontario, the Patti Starr Affair contributed to the downfall of the Peterson government.

Sir John A. Macdonald had Sir Hugh Allan and the famous election telegram, "I must have another ten thousand," which the prime minister promptly received.

Laurier caught a whiff of railway scandal with the promoters, MacKenzie and Mann.

Mackenzie King weathered the Beauharnois Scandal in which, in his own words, his government went through the "valley of the shadow."

On a minor note, one of Mackenzie King's ministers, according to Parliament Hill gossip, ran a call girl service out of his office.

And, what with the Rivard Affair and others equally sensational, the Pearson government seemed wreathed in scandal.

The Trudeau government had the Sky Shoppes, a cloud no bigger than a man's hand. In the Petrofina purchase, when the Trudeau government decided to go into the oil business by setting up PetroCanada, a finder's fee of one million dollars went to a friend of the party.

I have always had great difficulty in justifying a federal government presence in the operation of gas stations.

A flurry of market activity around the Petrofina sale, in which some persons close to the action made substantial profits, cast a shadow over the transaction. Trudeau responded by setting up a committee of public servants who duly—and dutifully—reported that all had proceeded with the utmost probity.

In the case of the Mulroney government, scandal appeared to be the name of the game as the government stumbled out of one mess and into another, paying a high price in the daily Question Period for the indiscretions of its members.

One Quebec MP, facing fraud charges by the RCMP for putting non-existent workers on his House of Commons payroll, called and asked what he should do.

I said, "Resign."

"And if I don't?"

"You'll be kicked out."

He thanked me and hung up.

A few moments later, someone from the Langevin Building called to rake me over the coals for talking to Quebec MPs.

I said, "I'll speak to any MP who phones and asks for my advice."

"You have no business doing that. I'll complain to the PM."

I never heard any more.

A Liberal member put a question on the House Order Paper demanding information about the salaries of people in the PMO. Two

Shirley Van Dusen, with granddaughter Grace, Tom and Brian Mulroney at the Aircraft Museum in Ottawa.

of the people he asked about had numbered bank accounts. I was the other. There was no secret about my bank account. I called a friend in the Press Gallery and asked him to drop over.

I gave him the facts about my salary, down to the last cent; my account at the Royal Bank on Sparks Street, in Ottawa (it was overdrawn); my bank loan; my mortgaged house in the country. I showed him everything.

"At least one guy in the Gallery will have the facts when the boys start reaching for a hot story."

Nothing ever happened. In a day or two, the question about me was removed from the House Order Paper; the others were not. I have always found straight talk is the best approach with the media. And anyone else, for that matter.

Inside the Tent

Chapter 23

With Mulroney in Barbados

I WAS SITTING in my office under the Peace Tower, behind John Diefenbaker's old desk looking out the window at the snow whipping across Parliament Hill. The Chief's statue, behind the West Block, was epauletted in white.

Visuals were chasing themselves through my brain: soothing vistas of golden beaches and palm trees, steel drums and rum punches.

I discovered the prime minister was going to Barbados to address a CARICOM meeting. CARICOM is important, since it represents the island nations of the Commonwealth, nations with which Canada has traded advantageously for three hundred years.

Motivated by a sense of pure patriotism, knowing that I was having lunch that day with the PM, I decided I should do something to bring to reality the tropical visions dancing in my head. The snow, whipping in malevolent sheets across the front of the Centre Block, helped to confirm my decision.

The prime minister sat in the Chief's old place in the alcove of the Parliamentary Restaurant overlooking the Ottawa River, now carapaced in ice. Up here, the snow was even more depressing. I broached the subject.

"I understand, Prime Minister, you're going to Barbados."

"That's right. Want to come along?"

"Very much, sir. It's possible I might be of help."

"I'm sure of it. We're leaving on the seventeenth of March, so it couldn't be more appropriate."

Both Quebec Irish, we spoke in a shorthand that would have meant nothing to anyone else.

I told Greg Guthrie I was hopping down to Barbados with the PM and suggested he join me. I would stay over for ten days after the conference. Peter Morgan, who had just left as Barbados High Commissioner to Canada, said we could use his place on the beach. I said only on condition we paid the going rate. I had no desire to see my picture in the *Globe and Mail*.

Guthrie, who in his early days had been a sugar planter in Guyana and before the war had sailed the Caribbean, jumped at the idea.

Then I discovered the trip also included a week in Mexico, where the PM was exploring trade possibilities. I brushed up on Mexican background, so when the official Canadian government aircraft put down in Mexico City, I was able to point dramatically at a distant snow-clad peak and exclaim in a loud voice,

"Popocateptl."

This made a tremendous impression on the surrounding Mexicans.

It seemed to leave the PM baffled.

We raced through Mexico City at break-neck speed to the luxurious Camino Real Hotel, where I found myself in a suite with a marble-floored bathroom complete with glass-walled tub, a bedroom with two double beds and a colour television with American programs, and a balcony looking down on a terrace where armed security guards leaped out and pointed automatic carbines every time I appeared.

I devoutly hoped they were guards and not bandits.

When I went down the hall, lounging guards, also armed with automatic carbines, watched me walk by with unfathomable eyes. I made a point of saying, "Buenas dias," just to let them know I was friendly. They seemed to appreciate my courtesy.

We went nowhere in Mexico City unless escorted by both motorcycle cops and soldiers. I wondered if there was a revolution pending. The soldiers wore steel helmets, green uniforms and expressionless faces which they must have lifted from the monuments that appear on every corner. There was no doubt in my mind that the soldiers were Aztecs. At a ceremony in the National Museum, where Aztec faces in stone also looked out from every corner, I asked a

Mexican official of obviously Spanish descent if there were any Aztecs left. He shook his head.

"All extinct."

I found this interesting, since there were about three million people with Aztec faces, not counting the soldiers, wandering round in Mexico City. Some may have been Toltecs, or Mayas. They are simply lumped together as *Indios*.

I distinguished myself at a banquet thrown by the president of Mexico by asking an attractive woman at the same table if she spoke French or Spanish. When she shook her head, I asked, "How about English?"

"Yes. I'm American."

You never know who you're talking to on these junkets.

While Mexico City is historic and exciting, I was happy when we took off, headed for the Caribbean.

It was here the PM called me up to his compartment at the front of the aircraft and asked me to read a rather long letter on the constitutional issue. The letter took strong exception to arguments against the Meech Lake Accord during an appearance before a Senate Committee by former Prime Minister Pierre Elliott Trudeau.

I am one of those who has a great deal of respect for Pierre Trudeau as a person, a politician and, above all, a highly qualified constitutional expert. After all, the man wrote it, didn't he? He was not, in my estimation, someone to mess around with.

I read the letter carefully and turned to face the PM. Mila was in the seat across, reading a magazine. She looked up. The PM said:

"This is a letter Joe Clark is sending to the *Toronto Star*."

"I wouldn't advise it."

"What do you mean?"

"Trudeau will tear this letter apart, Prime Minister. This is right up his alley. This is handing it to him on a plate."

"Would you like some coffee?"

We had coffee and I rose to go back to my seat. In the doorway, I paused.

"Has Joe Clark read this letter, Prime Minister?"

Mulroney gave me a hard look.

"As a matter of fact, no."

I went back to my seat beside David Halton of the CBC, feeling a little sorry for Joe Clark.

At Grantley Adams Airport in Barbados, the red carpet was out, quite literally, for Brian and Mila. I saw Peter Morgan with the Barbados Cabinet as they came forward to greet Canada's prime minister. I hung back, not wanting to interfere with the festivities.

Later, at a meeting with the Barbados government, Mulroney said, "There's no point in discussing anything, gentlemen, Van Dusen and Morgan have made all the decisions."

This brought a laugh, and no wonder.

One thing I did do at the CARICOM meetings, however, was suggest to the PM that we forgive the $80 million owed to Canada in repayment for CIDA loans, plus the accompanying interest at the rather high rates prevailing. My argument was simple. The CARICOM countries were strapped for cash as it was; as were a number of South American countries, whose loans had virtually doubled because of the high rates imposed under the previous government. There was no way they could pay back these huge obligations without breaking their shaky economies.

I wasn't sure how much remained to be paid, but I knew from my own observation on many of the islands that people were living in tin-roofed shacks. I knew the Americans had lent the islands $110 million and, at the same time, had imposed a sugar quota to protect their own beet growers. This was giving with one hand and taking away with the other.

Putting the whole matter in simple terms, we weren't going to get the money. Putting pressure on would defeat the purpose for which the loan was made in the first place: to assist Caribbean nations who bought a lot of goods from Canada and with whom Canada had been doing business for three centuries. So, why not forgive the loans and get the credit?

Mulroney announced he was going to do exactly that. And, predictably, the media, the only infallible force left in the world, now that doubt has been cast on the Pope, jumped all over him.

The Caribbean countries were, naturally, ecstatic.

I was standing outside the conference quarters when Prime Minister Michael Manley of Jamaica rushed out, grabbed a passing mike and intoned that Brian Mulroney was a great friend of the Caribbean and Canada the most generous country in the world. The same refrain was taken up by others. Had Brian Mulroney been able to run in the Caribbean, he would have won in a sweep.

That night at a reception at Sam Lord's Castle, the PM came up and said in a confidential tone.

"That Joe Clark letter. It's been toned down considerably. You'll like it."

The letter, toned down, as the PM said, appeared in the *Toronto Star* after we got back. Trudeau ignored it completely.

Good Fellows Get Together. Greg Guthrie, former Ottawa Journal reporter and assistant to John Diefenbaker, and Tom Van Dusen get together in the Government Lobby of Parliament with Joe Clark's Minister of Multiculturalism, Steve Paproski.

Meanwhile, I decided to give Guthrie a call at the beach house.

"I'll send a car down to pick you up for the reception."

"Where will you get a car?"

"Leave it to me, Guthrie."

I had taken steps to ingratiate myself with the people in charge of arrangements. I gave strict instructions to the driver who was going down to the beach house.

"Walk right up to the door and ask in a loud voice for Major Guthrie."

If there is one thing guaranteed to infuriate Guthrie, it is to be addressed by his wartime rank.

The driver did as directed and Guthrie arrived at the reception given by the Prime Minister of Barbados to be greeted by Mulroney like a long-lost brother.

The room was swarming with Caribbean prime ministers. One distinguished gentleman came up to me and said, "I'm the Prime Minister of the Virgins."

I immediately introduced him to the Prime Minister of Canada, who wisely refrained from any comment.

Chapter 24

The Parliament Buildings

IT'S A WORLD of its own, the Hill. East, Centre and West Blocks forming a protective arch around the interests of the Canadian people, the Peace Tower rising up from the ashes of the disastrous fire in 1916 to give a country then at war hope for better times.

Lavish portraits of former leaders line long corridors in the Centre Block leading to the Library, knowing and solemn in its Victorian pomposity. When I first went up to the Hill, the Parliamentary Library was a cosy, friendly place. MPs, ministers' aides and even reporters were encouraged to browse among the bookshelves under the benevolent and efficient administration of parliamentary librarian, F.A. Hardy. All that changed with the introduction of "Library Science." Members, perhaps with reason, were encouraged to stay out of the stacks.

In the basement of the West and Centre Blocks, the noisy hubbub of the cafeterias contrasts with the cool elegance of the Parliamentary Restaurant sitting serenely on the sixth floor of the Centre Block. From the windows a glittering view of Ottawa seduces the eye. The Rideau Canal—testament to the engineering genius of Colonel John By—sedately steps down to converge with the rollicking lumber chute of the Ottawa River. A spidery length of bridge joins the two solitudes of Ontario and Quebec under the unblinking gaze of Samuel de Champlain, his astrolabe held high as he charts the course for a new country. At his feet, an Algonquin chief peers into the great roiling kettle of the Chaudière Falls.

When visiting Canada in 1861, English novelist Anthony Trollope waxed lyrical about the prospect and design of the parliament buildings, then under construction, and about Parliament Hill itself.

> The view from the back of the Library up to the Chaudière Falls and the sawmills by which they are surrounded is very lovely. So that I will say again, that I know of no site for such a set of buildings so happy as regards both beauty and grandeur.

This was John Diefenbaker's favourite prospect, which he viewed at lunch in the first alcove overlooking the Ottawa River in the Parliamentary Restaurant.

The Liberals usually ate in a private dining room at the back of the restaurant. Not the Chief. Diefenbaker moved his cabinet out in full view of the entire dining room. In those days, the House sat at night and Mike Starr, Minister of Labour, sometimes invited me to join the cabinet table for dinner.

The cabinet table has now grown to two and there are also caucus tables where party members dine together. Then, of course, there are private tables where minions of the media hold forth with one ear cocked on the acoustics. For the Parliamentary Restaurant is notorious as a purveyor of secrets via the echo chambers of the shallow, saucer-shaped ceiling vaults.

In the Centre Block, Canada's history is revealed to the keen of eye through intricate carvings that cover the walls, arches and ceilings. One of the familiar night-time sounds is the chatter of the sculptor's chisel. Alive in stone, these masterpieces show glimpses of Canada's beauty, from the vast Arctic tundra to the tumbled waters of the Grand Banks. And some are startlingly familiar. Among the grinning gargoyles and facial masks are likenesses of those who lived and worked on the Hill. I often look up over the old Reading Room doorway to see Grattan O'Leary, quizzical as in life, touchstone to immortality.

In the East Block, Sir John A. Macdonald's old office has been restored as though waiting his return, with his desk, writing table, leather-covered chairs—even the stove—all in their familiar places.

Something went out of parliament when the traditional over-sized, overstuffed, leather-covered sofas were replaced with modern pieces, upholstered in floral fabrics. Thus was notice served that parliament was no longer a male preserve.

Sir Wilfrid Laurier's office also patiently awaits his reappearance in the East Block. It is preserved just as when he worked there. One expects him to rise and come forward, hand outstretched, welcoming visitors with his famous smile.

Trudeau and Mulroney preferred the third-floor office in the Centre Block, one flight up from the Commons Chamber. Diefenbaker used the fourth-floor office favoured by Mackenzie King, away from the hurly burly of crowded corridors and the Public Gallery.

Technically, the prime minister has two offices on the Hill. Traditionally, one was in the Centre Block near the Chamber and one in the East Block. When Pierre Trudeau was prime minister, the East Block was undergoing renovations, so he moved off the Hill, where the prime minister had had his office since the days of Laurier, across Wellington Street to the Langevin Building. The Prime Minister's Office remains there to this day. When I was a young reporter on the *Ottawa Journal*, Louis St Laurent was in the East Block, as was the Cabinet Room. The Cabinet later moved over to the third floor of the Centre Block.

During the 1916 fire, the old bell, in a somewhat shorter and stubbier tower, tolled out the alarm and came crashing to the ground. Speaker Albert Sevigny managed to escape down a ladder with his wife, who was two months pregnant at the time with a future minister in a Diefenbaker government, the Honourable Pierre Sevigny. Unfortunately, two of Speaker Sevigny's guests were not so lucky and were asphyxiated.

That same night, Grattan O'Leary, who was enjoying his first success as a young reporter on the *Ottawa Journal*, was attending a dinner next door at the Château Laurier in honour of Sir Sam Hughes, Minister of Militia. He managed to get up to the burning Centre Block and rescue his typewriter, in those days, a reporter's first concern.

At one time, Parliament Hill hummed at all hours of the day and night, sometimes to the skirl of the Honourable Tom Reid's pipes. A senator from New Westminster, British Columbia, he liked to pace the marble halls dressed in kilt and sporran, evoking images of a

Scottish past. Under the Trudeau government, the rules were changed to end night sittings—why, it has never been made quite clear—casting a pall over the House after six o'clock. Where previously the House had been a place of bustling animation, with members busy in their offices or entertaining colleagues and guests in the restaurant, and even senators moving at measured pace through the halls, it now takes on the appearance of an Etruscan tomb as the sun sinks below the Gatineau Hills.

Only silence is left to stalk the halls, broken occasionally by the footfall of a security guard on his rounds. The House is dark and empty—like a medieval monastery—no longer a forum for great after-dinner speeches, with eloquence reinforced by an after-dinner drink.

Speeches now are considerably flatter and staler. There was a time when members, and even ministers, formed their own thoughts and delivered them in their own words. This was before an army of PR experts and speech writers settled like locusts on the halls of parliament.

While it is true the House is a little more conscious of decorum now, with television exposure and the presence of women MPs, it does not hold for Question Period when some female members, like Sheila Copps, out-do the male members in toughness and stridency.

Sheila is not really that way. As a young reporter on the *Ottawa Citizen*, she sometimes came out to our house in Aylmer with Mark and Tom, our sons, both of whom also worked for the *Citizen*. She was a quiet, attractive girl. In personal conversation, she still is. Sheila's father, Vic Copps, was mayor of Hamilton and a noted political figure. Her uncle, Eddie Copps, was a *Time* magazine reporter. Sheila has both politics and media in her blood. Sometimes it seems she is trying to reassure the ghost of her dead father that he did the right thing in having a girl. Sheila can do all the things boys can. And better.

Security forms an important part of parliament. Trudeau introduced the bullet-proof limousine with outriders. Under Brian Mulroney, this was enlarged to include an accompanying aircraft when the prime minister travelled to foreign parts. What a contrast from the days when Sir Wilfrid Laurier took a streetcar from his home to the Hill and Louis St Laurent walked down Elgin Street to his apartment in the old Roxborough.

Then there was the case of the Nova Scotia member, a former fisherman, who decided he could live in his office in the House, rather than spend money on an apartment in town. When the Speaker found out about it, he summarily evicted the penny-pinching Maritimer.

A group of Alberta members in the Diefenbaker government ran into a similar restriction when they decided to barbecue in the office. In spite of tissues stuffed in the mail slot and around the door, there was no hiding the aroma of roasting Alberta beef drifting down the hall. Once again, the sergeant-at-arms was sent to do his duty, warning the members to cease and desist.

An Eastern Ontario member who made a habit of a morning roll in the hay with his secretary was somewhat nonplussed when, in the middle of the action, his phone rang and a voice said, "God is watching." The call came from a bunch of Press Gallery reporters who had discovered an alcove whose windows looked down on the member's office, providing an intimate view of the goings-on inside.

As the Chief used to say, parliament is "an asylum run by the inmates."

Those were the days before MPs enjoyed research staffs and private offices. Most members shared secretaries from the pool. Old-timers received what were then regarded as privileges—private offices and personal secretaries. Now all MPs demand full amenities as perks of office, while their predecessors worked harder and did more with less. They filled the usual complement of committees and sat until ten o'clock at night to complete the day's work. The argument in favour of higher salaries, gaudy pensions and enlarged staffs was that a better calibre of member would be elected.

It would be a brave analyst indeed who would suggest that the calibre has risen noticeably since Robert Borden came to parliament, or Wilfrid Laurier, or Ernest Lapointe, or John Diefenbaker. There has, however, been a noticeable rise in the education level of MPs, which is probably just a reflection of what has been going on in the country. But, conversely, there is a noticeable drop in the regard Canadians once held for their representatives. It's an opinion I don't share. By and large, today's politicians are decent, well-intentioned people, much like the voters they represent.

Parliament is, after all, a forum where the views of ordinary citizens receive an airing. It doesn't demand rocket scientists or microbiologists, but rather men and women capable of representing the views of their constituents in a context of the greater good for the greater number.

It is true the buildings clustered on the Hill represent much that is hopeful in Canadian life. If changes are to come, in the shape of better representation for the unrepresented and under-represented, they will come in the House of Commons. The buildings are the cradle of the nation, built at the time of Confederation to house the new democracy, contemporaneous with Canada, maturing with the nation. Here, Canadians bring their children to see democracy's face.

My view of the Hill is not the familiar postcard picture: the Peace Tower looming against white, woolly clouds and red-jacketed guards going through intricate manoeuvres on emerald-green lawns. No, I picture the Hill as I've so often seen it, walking down on a winter evening, with swatches of snow blurring the Peace Tower clock and lamps dim in the snowy night.

CHAPTER 25

Goodbye, Again

EVERYTHING comes to an end.

By 1991, my duties in the Prime Minister's Office began to have a sameness about them. The raucous belly-aching in the House took on the appearance of a bad play too long running. I became aware of creeping boredom.

I suppose, however, my job was unique.

I had an office on Parliament Hill, which had once belonged to a Liberal minister. I had a secretary. I had a paycheque that came every couple of weeks. And I had a view of the Centre Block lawn and a ringside seat to all the demonstrations.

I got to see the prime minister nearly every day. And every now and then, he took me to lunch. And, every day, I sent him a memo, giving him a rundown on what the media were saying and the political implications thereof.

The title on my tastefully printed business cards read "Caucus Liaison."

I did some of that, too. I had been around Ottawa a long time, around the Hill a long time, and around the Press Gallery and media a long time. Some people thought too long.

I had been in and out of the public service over the years, in a gaggle of government information offices and a muddle of ministers' offices; some Liberal, some Conservative. Have typewriter, will travel.

When people speculated on the nature of my job, I sometimes thought of a large, stuffed owl on a staircase in a house in Westport on Upper Rideau Lake. The house belonged to a friend and supporter of

Sir John A. Macdonald. When Sir John was too tired or indisposed—or taken in strong drink—he would stay overnight at Foley's before going on to Kingston. As a reward, he made Foley Postmaster General.

But this isn't about Foley.

It's about the stuffed owl on Foley's landing, still there to this day.

The owl represents continuity.

It is exciting to know Sir John A. saw that owl every time he went up or down the stairs. Sometimes, he may not have seen the owl too clearly; but he always knew the owl was there.

That was my function with the government of Brian Mulroney. To represent continuity with the past and the great men who had gone on before.

Like the owl on the staircase.

I would be turning seventy that August, however. So, although I have never been one to worry about chronology, this was one I couldn't slough off. If I was going to do something with my life, I had to get started.

I wanted to finish my novel on the War of 1812—the war Canada won.

There were a lot of books I wanted to read.

There were things I wanted to know more about. Like the Cosmos.

When you have spent forty-five years with your nose on a white chalkline, you wonder what will happen when you look up.

I had wood to cut at our place in Russell on the Castor River, near Ottawa. I had grass to cut. Things to do.

I wanted to sit on the sand in Barbados, watch the green sea roll up to my feet, read Mark Twain and O. Henry, gaze at the great, golden doubloon of the Caribbean moon, listen to the Trade Winds rustling in the palms, and drink rum punch.

I wanted to be at the Cacrabank at six o'clock when the retired colonels come out on the deck and raise their glasses as the crimson sun plunges into the sea.

Sure, it would be tough. And stressful.

But I would survive.

At the Chief's feet. Tom Van Dusen at the foot of John Diefenbaker's statue on Parliament Hill.

About the Authors

Tom Van Dusen

Tom Van Dusen worked as an aide for John Diefenbaker, Robert Stanfield, Erik Nielsen and Michael Starr, Diefenbaker's Minister of Labour. He also worked for Allan J. MacEachen, Pierre Trudeau's President of the Privy Council, and Mitchell Sharpe. He retired after spending ten years in the office of Brian Mulroney. His slogan: "Have Typewriter, Will Travel."

A former member of the Parliamentary Press Gallery, Van Dusen is the author of *The Chief* and *The Power Brokers*.

Born in Ottawa, Van Dusen grew up in Gracefield, Quebec, where his grandfather, Thomas Grace, kept a general store. He received his primary education in a one-room village schoolhouse before going on to graduate from the University of Ottawa with a bachelor's degree in Arts and Philosophy.

Van Dusen is a keen frequenter of the Caribbean and spends as much time as he can among the islands he first visited in the company of John Diefenbaker.

His wife, Shirley Van Dusen, is a well-known artist who has painted former Speaker of the House of Commons, John Bosley, the Mulroney children and the son and daughter-in-law of former Governor General Jeanne Sauvé. Their seven children are prominent in broadcasting and communications.

Susan Code

Susan Code has enjoyed a peripatetic career as—among other things—a writer, editor, historical interpreter, assistant to a cabinet minister and college instructor, while living in her home town of Perth, Ontario. She holds an honours degree in History from Queen's University at Kingston and is the author of *A Matter of Honour and Other Tales of Early Perth* (General Store Publishing House 1996).

To order more copies of

INSIDE THE TENT
FORTY-FIVE YEARS ON
PARLIAMENT HILL

send $19.95 plus $5.05
to cover GST, shipping and handling to:

GENERAL STORE PUBLISHING HOUSE
1 Main Street, Burnstown, Ontario
K0J 1G0

(613) 432-7697 or **1-800-465-6072**
Fax 613-432-7184
URL – http://www.gsph.com.